YOU ARE WHAT YOU EAT,
WEAR, DRIVE, LIVE IN
AND CHOOSE AS A PET!

Aided by a fascinating collection of case histories, Dr. Jean Rosenbaum shows how we
can assess the profoundest personality traits
in each other and in ourselves.

*IS YOUR VOLKSWAGEN A SEX
SYMBOL?*
breaks the code that deciphers the real you!

Is
Your
Volkswagen
a Sex Symbol?

By Jean Rosenbaum, M.D.

BANTAM BOOKS

TORONTO · NEW YORK · LONDON

A NATIONAL GENERAL COMPANY

*This low-priced Bantam Book
has been completely reset in a type face
designed for easy reading, and was printed
from new plates. It contains the complete
text of the original hard-cover edition.*
NOT ONE WORD HAS BEEN OMITTED.

IS YOUR VOLKSWAGEN A SEX SYMBOL?
*A Bantam Book / published by arrangement with
Hawthorn Books, Inc.*

PRINTING HISTORY
Hawthorn edition published June 1972
2nd printing .... July 1972
3rd printing ...... August 1972
4th printing ...... August 1972
Literary Guild edition published February 1973
Bantam edition published August 1973

*Bantam Books are published by Bantam Books, Inc., a National
General company. Its trade-mark, consisting of the words "Bantam
Books" and the portrayal of a bantam, is registered in the United
States Patent Office and in other countries. Marca Registrada.
Bantam Books, Inc., 666 Fifth Avenue, New York, N.Y. 10019.*

PRINTED IN THE UNITED STATES OF AMERICA

Preface

What deep psychological forces cause us to select the kind of car we have, the pets we treasure, the house we love, and our very manners and ways of doing things? Why do we prefer one thing over another anyway? What forces us without our knowledge to select blondes over brunettes, to pick the kind of job we have, the clothes we wear, the way we shake hands, even the types of fun and recreation we enjoy? Are these things accidental, coincidental, due only to outside influence? It might be comfortable to view them in this way, but this is not the case at all.

Everything a person does, especially those things that he has done so often that they become automatic, is deeply meaningful. The reasons you doodle the things you do while on the telephone, undertip or overtip, or even pursue the hobby you love may not be known to you. It is also unlikely that you know what these things reveal about you, either to yourself or to others. The trained eye, however, can obtain a great deal of information about your makeup from observing them.

Early in my teaching experience I became a specialist in the quick emergency psychiatric interview. I learned to be able to tell what I needed to know about the person being interviewed within a very few minutes and oftentimes without his conscious cooperation. Was this magic? Did I have some special intuition that others didn't possess? Certainly not. But this kind of reduced-clues observation turned out to be so reliable that I became quite in demand to teach this kind of personality-scanning technique to psychiatrists in training.

The purpose of this book is not to make you self-conscious or to equip you to put other people on the spot; but our habits, choices, and preferences do tell a great deal about our personalities, and learning to decipher the clues can lead to important revelations. I am not speaking here just about the superficial personality you show to others, for more often than not it is a screen that protects the real you. Rather, I am talking about your personality structure—what really makes you tick.

Everything a person is can be found in the message conveyed by his manners and habits. Your habits, indeed, tell all. Let's see if we can decode the message.

J. R.

Contents

Is
Your
Volkswagen
a Sex Symbol?

1

Is More Horsepower Really
More Happiness?

THE AUTOMOBILE, A NATIONAL SYMBOL AND A SUBCULTURE

Instead of the eagle, the national symbol of the United States should be the automobile, for the nation has become the land of pistons and the home of horsepower. The automobile is as symbolic of our new technological era as the cowboy's horse was in the rugged frontier days.

Although the automobile is only one of our major technological advances, it has revolutionized our way of living and has had a tremendous psychological effect on our lives. In a very real emotional sense the automobile has become synonymous with happiness.

Why is the automobile so important? Why has it become such a strong force in our culture? It has far surpassed all its predecessors in its emotional hold on people and its psychological impact on both society and the individual. Henry Ford said he invented the automobile because he was a lazy man. That statement puts the finger on one

1

of the chief attractions of the automobile and the reason for its continued popularity: The automobile is the number-one answer for the lazy man who lives within nearly all of us. This lazy man, who has little or no regard for the muscular or motor functions of the body, is the reason we continually look for easier ways of doing things. The automobile not only has catered to that laziness but in some ways has strengthened it. If doing things the easy way has become part of the national syndrome, it is partly because of the convenience of the automobile.

The automobile, however, is more than a convenience; it is a symbol. Owning and driving a car are a sign of adulthood, though not necessarily a sign of mature and responsible adulthood. It is a symbol of belonging to a group, and it brings group recognition. This is so much the case that persons who don't own or drive a car frequently feel on the defensive—that they must offer some explanation to others for this behavioral aberration.

"I should learn to drive," a colleague said apologetically as he asked for a ride home from a meeting, "but I've always been too busy, and besides, I lived in the city for so many years where I just used public transportation."

Another friend told me that she had felt forced to take driving lessons even though she had no car.

"I was so embarrassed because I didn't have a driver's license," she explained. "Whenever I wanted to cash a check, the clerk would ask to see my driver's license. When I said I didn't have one, she would look disbelievingly at me. It made me feel guilty. Really, I felt like a second-class citizen!"

In another instance a man said that his friends and relatives made him feel like a failure because he did not own a car.

"They assume," he complained, "that I am either financially unable to purchase one or too incompetent to own one."

These are almost classic cases of individual self-esteem being lowered because of social pressure and group disapproval.

Although it is difficult to ignore the automobile, some people try to and do, to an extent, succeed in organizing their life-style in at least a semi-nonautomotive pattern. Such people are usually opposed to technology, and they like to pick and choose modern conveniences, discarding or ignoring those they dislike or disapprove of. Because of the psychological and sociological implications surrounding them, automobiles have become particular objects of disdain.

It has even become the "in" thing among some intellectuals to adopt a pseudoprimitivism and denigrate the place of automobiles in modern life. There is a big scrap heap in these people's minds to which they consign automobiles, television sets, and elaborate and (to them) unnecessary household appliances and gadgets.

Ben, a successful artist, is very scornful of automobiles. He does not own a car and does not know how to drive. He has even converted his garage into a storeroom. Ben rides a bicycle or walks. However, if you offer him a lift in bad weather, he forgets his prejudices against automobiles and is happy to get into the warmth and comfort of a car.

There have always been various influential subcultures in this country; however, no subculture has been so strong or exerted so much influence as the automobile subculture. Immediately preceding it was what we could call the frontier or pioneer subculture. This was the dream of the eighteenth and nineteenth centuries that held people enthralled and united the efforts of the entire nation. There are a number of important differences between that subculture and the automobile subculture. The frontier subculture was indigenous in its nature, basically creative, and one of mutual participation and growth. It was a constructive, life-building subculture. The automobile subculture is an imposed one, which is consumer-oriented. Basically artificial, it is structured toward the individual and toward destructiveness.

It is almost impossible to escape its implications and effects if you live in the United States. You are surrounded by it, and your daily life is influenced by it. You do not even have to own an automobile or be able to drive one to become an integral part of it. Automobiles and superhighways have become the common factors uniting people and dominant factors in city planning, industrial locations, and other commercial ventures. The automobile has changed our habits and customs—go through any town of any size and you can see evidence of the automobile subculture: drive-in banks, movies, and restaurants and mobile-home parks. It has even changed the landscape. Miles of concrete, cloverleaf interchanges, huge directional signs, and gasoline stations have become the new "country." Gas stations are now like the old temples of the oracles. You stop at the stations not only for gasoline but for your own personal needs, to ask for directions, for suggestions on where to go, where to stay, and where to eat.

The modern gasoline station gives you all the comfort and succor you need. You can drive away with a full tank for your car and a contented feeling for yourself. The attendant has waited on you, talked to you, and perhaps even admired your automobile. You may have had a soft drink or a candy bar and received a free map. If you had a breakdown, you consider a good mechanic as necessary as a good doctor.

In any social gathering you can get people to talk more enthusiastically about their choice of gas stations and gasoline brands than about their churches and religions.

"Why not?" exclaimed one man when this point was discussed. "My car is my lifeline to my work, my home, and my fun. If it breaks down, then I'm in *real* trouble!"

However, another breakdown that threatens us is the total breakdown of the automobile subculture because of overcrowding and overpopulation. Today man faces a strange dilemma, for while on the one hand he has created automobiles, by the millions, on the other hand he has created giant cities, and the city is the natural enemy of the automobile.

Overcrowding and urban congestion have combined to defeat the very purposes for which the automobile was built, sold, and bought. Of what possible use is a 350-horsepower, four-speed-transmission car when you can only crawl along at five to ten miles an hour in low-gear stop-and-go driving in rush-hour traffic? And when you do get to your destination, what do you do about parking? The plain truth is that there is no longer room in the large cities for private automobiles.

THE AUTOMOBILE AS AN EXTENSION AND EXPRESSION OF THE PERSONALITY

Unlike the airplane, the automobile is a mass product for the ordinary person. Economically it is within the reach of most people. Airplanes would have even more impact on our social culture and life-style if they became as common as automobiles. A small, easily handled, and inexpensive machine such as a type of helicopter or flying platform would dramatically change man's concept of himself. Once the average citizen can fly as casually as he now drives, he will have a more intensified sense of mastery over his limitations. It will be one more step on the long path to reach out beyond his original capabilities.

Man is unique in this desire. A dog sees a bird fly, but he does not try, even over generations, to learn to fly. A man sees a bird fly and decides that he, too, will fly. And he works by trial and error to discover a means of doing it. It is this "divine discontent" that has taken men over the centuries from chariot to car, to airplane, to spaceship.

Perhaps the biggest psychological basis and compensation for owning an automobile is that the automobile has become an extension of the individual personality. It has become the means by which man is able to actively express his wishes for power and mastery over nature. Although there are many inventions that have helped to make man's life easier, the automobile has been the main source of man's advancement beyond himself. No longer is he bound to one place or limited to slow, arduous travel. He can conquer hours and thereby lengthen his time of influence.

Choices of cars and attitudes toward them can be very revealing. Traits such as aggression, dependence, fearfulness, independence, and superiority are shown through automobiles. A timid, dependent person will drive a medium-size or small car, or he or she may refuse to drive at all. The openly aggressive person will use his automobile to work off his feelings of hostility. The person who feels that he cannot be openly aggressive will use his automobile to express his aggressiveness through passive actions. These actions are negative in their intent and are merely repressed or disguised expressions of hostility. We classify such a person as one having a passive-aggressive personality.

Fred, an older Negro, had that type of personality. He was what young blacks call an Uncle Tom. To whites, he was very servile, but he was repressing a strong feeling of hatred. That hatred was expressed whenever he got into his automobile and went out on the highway, for in his car he felt not just equal, but a little superior, although still afraid to act too openly and display this feeling. How did he show his passive-aggressive personality in driving? Picture the rush hour: Traffic is heavy, and people are anxious to get home, but there is an obstacle—Fred. Fred is driving in the left-hand lane of the freeway or sometimes even in the middle of the road, and he is driving at least ten miles below the speed limit. He is holding up traffic with the rear end of his automobile. In a sense he is sticking his own rear end in other people's faces. Fred had been reared and had lived most of his adult life in a cultural and political milieu where any overt expression of aggression or hostility might be met with punishment, even death. For this reason he learned to adapt and express his anger at white people in a passive way. If you asked him why he was deliberately getting in the white man's way, Fred would deny that he was doing it. He would claim to be ignorant of any act of wrongdoing or malicious intent.

Attitudes of superiority, either real or imagined, are usually shown by the possession of a big car. For generations of Americans the symbol of wealth and power was the chauffeured limousine. The young secretary would sit in the movie house and see herself being helped into the big automobile by the chauffeur and seated at the side of the car's rich owner or better yet, his handsome son. In the same vein the clerk, the student, the mill hand, all dreamed of being able to say, "Home, James." Today chauffeurs are almost an anachronism, no longer a necessary symbol of wealth and power. The attitude of the wealthy has changed to include the idea of *not* having a car as a sign of their independence and freedom from financial concern.

The person who has a chauffeur in this day and age is an exhibitionist. Not only is he calling attention to himself and his wealth, but he is also convincing himself that he really is important. In effect he is saying that he has too much to do and too much to think about to be bothered with the details of driving. To this kind of person, *having* his money is the important thing, and any outward proof or demonstration of that money becomes equally important. This individual is one we would classify as an anal character. He is proud of his accumulation and retention of wealth. This is related to the young child's attitude toward his own feces as the measure of his importance. On the other hand the wealthy person who does not own a car may be more of a realist. He is interested in the creative aspects of earning money rather than in the possession of money or objects. His choice not to own a car may be based on the reasoning that it is more economical for him to rent a car. We would classify such an individual as a genital character. He gets a lot of excitement and fun out of life.

There are two other stages besides anal and genital—the phallic and the oral stages. The phallic stage in connection with automobiles will be discussed in greater detail later in this chapter. Phallic symbolism is a power symbolism—in particular, a symbol of male sexual domination. Oral symbolism is its opposite. Oral symbolism calls to mind the dependence of childhood. It is a reminder of helplessness. The oral character frequently places himself in the position of victim.

In automobiles oral qualities are considered negative qualities. For example a car that is not a good car is one that "eats" a lot of gas or oil. Men do not want to associate oral qualities with their cars, for it does not fit their self-image of being strong and virile. It was just this sort of oral symbolism that was responsible for the failure of the Edsel. The physical appearance of the Edsel was displeasing from a psychological and emotional point of view because the front grille looked like a huge open mouth. For this reason the Edsel became known as The Mouth in automobile-manufacturing circles. Clinical and automotive-industry studies showed this to be a major cause for its lack of popularity. People prefer their cars to be sex or power symbols rather than symbols of dependence.

AUTOMOBILES AS SEXUAL SYMBOLS

The automobile is the most common sex symbol in our modern society. It is identified with sexual ability and physical sexual characteristics. It is no accident that most young male car-owners get pleasure out of masturbating while in their cars. It is natural, therefore, that the automobile should be the setting for petting and sexual intercourse.

Sexual identification accounts for much of the popularity of sports cars and convertibles. An owner of such a car assumes people will say of him, "He's a real swinger!" Even the most staid personality may get a secret thrill out of owning and driving a sports car. What he is saying to the world and especially to women is, "Don't look at me, look at my car. That is the real me!" It would be more accurate if he said, "That is the me I wish I were."

The man who is emotionally well-adjusted and feels comfortable with himself and his masculinity is not overly concerned with automobiles. He is able to express his sexuality in a direct way. He does not need an external phallic or power symbol of any kind. His sexual security is not rooted in material objects. He is sure of himself. Therefore, automobiles have no special significance for him. Frequently this type of individual will have an old car, as reliable in its temperament and performance as is its owner.

Some individuals do not understand or wish to understand the phallic significance of the automobile. A patient consulted me because he would have an erection whenever he drove his car through a tunnel or under a bridge. He found this very disturbing because he did not understand it. As many individuals do, he had sexualized the objects around him. His automobile symbolized his penis, and any hollow opening unconsciously represented the vagina to him.

The automobile is a common symbol of female sexuality as well as a symbol of male sexuality. In this respect we could say that the automobile fulfills the role of psychological bisexuality, which makes it even more valuable to the average person as a means of expressing the varying needs of his sexual nature.

The automobile as a symbol progresses in the average male mind from a symbol of the womb to a symbol of woman. This follows along his own emotional development from dependence on his mother to an interest in girls and other women. Children under five years of age experience automobiles as a sort of pseudowomb. They feel contained and protected within the car, and thus they have a tendency to fall asleep when the car is moving. This is the satisfaction of an internal need. When the child grows up, this womb feeling becomes translated into more adult feelings. The adolescent now, instead of wanting to get into the womb of the mother for peace, wants to enter a woman for sexual satisfaction.

It is very common for the first sexual experience to occur in a car despite the fact that it is uncomfortable and risks discovery by the police or peeping toms. However, it seems the logical place because it represents the female interior.

All societies have some kind of puberty rites to mark the passage from childhood to adulthood. In the United States learning to drive, getting a driver's license, and getting an automobile are the equivalent of primitive puberty rites. Thus, when a boy is able to drive, he has presumably proved himself capable of manhood and can say, "Today I am a man!" The driver's license and the automobile become the external signs of his manhood. In primitive societies after the boy was initiated in some approved ritualistic way, he was given a spear or a bow and arrow. These implements signified his penis and his acceptance into tribal membership as an adult. Today the automobile takes the place of the weapon and symbolizes a functional penis and manhood.

In our society it is not permissible to discuss in mixed groups the size or potency of the penis, yet this is something most adolescents are interested in. Car chatter becomes a substitute. Boys will discuss the power and capability of automobiles, often bragging about the speed and special features of their own cars. Most girls do not understand the real meaning of car chatter and become exasperated.

"I'd like to talk about other things, but all he wants to talk about is his car!" is a frequent complaint.

The emotionally immature man who retains his adolescent sexual attitudes will often use the same conversational tactics and have the same adolescent attitudes toward his car. To him a car is more than a means of transportation; it is a symbol of his maleness.

Joe has a new car. It's the flashiest car he could get, and it's loaded with accessories. Joe wants to be sure that you notice him. He is an exhibitionist, a show-off personality. Some exhibitionists get in trouble because they can't resist calling attention to their sex organs, but exhibitionists like Joe are more subtle. To Joe, his flashy car is a symbol of his penis, and he wants to be sure that everybody notices it.

"Hey, look at me!" is what Joe says as he roars up to a stoplight and guns his motor while waiting for the light to change. Joe knows he annoys people, but he doesn't care. To be sure that he isn't overlooked, he has rolled his windows down and is playing the radio full blast. He is snapping his fingers and singing or whistling with the piece being played. The light changes, and Joe pulls away, leaving several inches of rubber on the road. You'd recognize Joe even if you saw him without his car. He's the kind who flexes his muscles in public, wears extreme clothes, and equates the length of the penis with strength and ability.

There is a link between sexual prowess and horsepower in the minds of most men, and they also tend to equate driving with sexual function. This leads to the assumption that the bigger the car—that is, the more horsepower—the greater the amount of happiness to be received and enjoyed. This ingenious theory is largely responsible for the sale and success of the big car.

In reality Mr. Average Driver never gets a chance to try out his horsepower. He can only brag about it, and he brags about it as a substitution for bragging about his sexual life. "See what a big car I have!" can be translated as "See what a big penis I have!" (or "wish I had") and "See what a great lover I am!"

Gilbert came to me for treatment of anxiety and tension. He was an insurance executive with a large company, had been married twenty-eight years, and on the surface, at least, appeared to have a very successful life. It was not easy for Gilbert to talk about his personal life, particularly his marriage. There was one subject, however, that he never seemed to tire of—his automobile. Gilbert drove a big car—in fact, one of the biggest available. In contrast to his evasiveness about his own life, he could and did talk at length about mileage, speed, horsepower, and related topics. It was only through analysis that Gilbert's real problem was revealed. He suffered from sexual impotency, a fact he tried to disguise by putting emphasis upon the power and performance of his automobile.

Automobiles are also part of our internal or psychic world; thus, dreams about automobiles are common. Sometimes, however, these dreams turn into nightmares when the dream automobile breaks down, its brakes fail, its lights do not work, or the tires go flat. Any of these occurrences in dreams is an indication of personal anxiety, fears, frustrations, or tension. A typical case was that of a young man who consulted me because he was having trouble relating to the opposite sex. It was difficult to get him to discuss his sexual feelings and attitudes, but in one session he mentioned a dream. In the dream he was driving his automobile along a modern highway which was surrounded by beautiful scenery. Suddenly his car began to wobble as the right front tire went flat. He was forced to stop driving. After relating this dream, he was persuaded to discuss his actual problem—fears regarding his sexual potency. These fears were based on an early experience when he had been unable to maintain an erection.

In a somewhat similar case an older man who feared sexual impotency had recurring dreams in which he was driving and ran out of gas.

Automobile manufacturers are very much aware of this sexual identification and use it in their advertisements. Pretty girls are shown surrounding the owner of X car. The man who buys a Y is suddenly overwhelmed by attractive women. A television commercial shows a man driving a Z make of automobile. He is handsome, suave, and debonair. As he steps from his Z, several women stop and give him and his automobile admiring glances. The implications of such advertisements are plain even to the most backward viewers.

So Mr. Average Man, who may be paunchy, middle-aged, bald, and disappointed in life, buys a Z car in the hope that it will change his life and bring him some excitement. It is a vain hope, although in some cases the mere ownership of a Z may compensate to some extent for an otherwise dull and unsatisfactory life.

In a recent Chevrolet commercial a Camaro is supposedly mistaken for a racing car, and the sheriff tells the driver he cannot have that kind of a car in town. It is, of course, a very racy-looking car with a long hood—phallic symbolism at its best.

In a Dodge commercial a milquetoast type is parked on the beach with his girl. He is trying to get up the courage to propose when suddenly the car is surrounded by a bevy of beautiful girls.

Early Mustang commercials put emphasis on the joyfulness of life and the possibilities of romance. Advertisements implied that your life would be changed if you only drove a Mustang. It was hinted that when you turned on the ignition key, you would also turn on popularity.

SELF-IMAGE AND HOW AND WHY YOU CHOOSE YOUR AUTOMOBILE

There are psychological reasons for choosing the automobile you do, and your choice of car may reflect exhibitionism, inferiority, family loyalty, delusions of grandeur, and other personality traits. Your choice reflects your self-image, for there is a tendency to make self-image and the external object, the automobile, correspond in some way. The how and why of your selection of an automobile are directly related to your ego, id, and superego.

In psychiatry we think of the mind as divided into three psychological parts: the ego, the id, and the superego. The ego, which is the most accessible part, is primarily conscious. It acts as a mediator between your internal drives and demands and the reality of your external environment with its demands. It is responsible for making compromises between your aggressive and sexual demands and the outside world. The id is part of your unconscious. It is the pleasure- and destruction-seeking region of the mind; basically, it is irresponsible. The superego is also mostly a part of your unconscious. It is the seat of your goals, ethics, and morals. Picture your mind as a courtroom: The id is the delinquent, the superego is judge and jury, and the ego is an overworked attorney.

How does all this relate to your automobile? If you own a car, it means that you have convinced yourself of the acceptability of what was once called this wondrous machine. Your superego makes this decision for you. It says to you, "Go ahead. Automobiles are good. Automobiles are desirable possessions. Automobiles are necessary." Obviously millions of superegos are saying that everyday and have been for a number of years. Why you want a car in the first place is an id function. It is a process of identification which is often sexual or aggressive. You have an automobile as an extension of your personality, as a concretization of your sexual desires and aggressive impulses.

Your ego controls the actual automobile-buying process, but your superego has to put its stamp of approval on that process. It decides what kind of an automobile you pick. You may select a car that you know will be approved by your parents or your boss, or you may choose on grounds of economy or other similar reasons.

The meek little man who sees himself as he is will buy and drive a small car. However, if he sees himself as a person of power or has fantasies and daydreams in which he is a leader, he will buy a big car even when it is an economic burden to him.

The timid individual wants an automobile that will not dominate him. He is frightened by horsepower, by a multiplicity of dials and guages, and by the sheer weight of the automobile. He tries to find a car that he can trust, just as a timid rider will ask for a slow and gentle horse. Or the selection may be a form of overcompensation. He may try to cover up a basic feeling of inferiority by buying an expensive car. Or it may reflect delusions of grandeur.

This was the case with George. He admitted that he was heavily in debt because he had purchased a car that was out of his financial range.

"It's also expensive to keep up," he said ruefully.

"But why did you buy it?"

"Well, I'm just a clerk, but I wish I were an executive. I thought maybe people would see me drive past and think I was a big shot."

Just as Peter Pan never wanted to grow up, so some persons refuse to accept adulthood responsibilities. A prolonged adolescence in terms of emotional immaturity can influence your selection of an automobile.

"I wish Arthur would buy a sensible car," his wife lamented. "We need a sedan, a family car, but he insists on getting a sports car. There are other things we need, but he insists that we have a new car every two years. We are always in debt. He's not happy unless he has the latest model!"

Arthur had never grown up. He retained his teen-age single-minded passion for fast cars, even though the purchase of such cars was hurting his family financially. He also did not stop to consider his family's comfort.

The realization of a desired image in other people's eyes can also be a factor in automobile purchase.

"I really liked my old car," a lawyer told me, "but I was afraid that people would think I couldn't afford a new one if I didn't get one."

"I was going to buy a red car," another man said, "but I live in a very conservative neighborhood, and I was afraid of what the neighbors might say, so I got a dark green one instead."

"I would like to drive a little sports car," a minister said, "but I'm sure my congregation wouldn't approve."

Family influences play an important role in automobile selection. A son may continue to purchase the same make of automobile that his father did if he still feels under the domination of his father.

"I'd like to get a Volkswagen," a neighbor told me, "but my father would have a fit. He has always driven a Chevrolet and thinks I should, too. It's just not worth a family fight."

MALE AND FEMALE ATTITUDES TOWARD BUYING AN AUTOMOBILE

Are there appreciable differences in the way men and women select their personal automobiles? I would say Yes. Women are more apt to be interested in style, color, and convenience of handling. They study various consumer ratings of automobiles. They also make inquiries about the performance of an automobile from relatives, friends, and the salesman. They are more willing to be guided in their selection. Women are probably shrewder buyers because they are less swayed by horsepower and nonessential accessories. They are accustomed to bargain hunting and are interested in getting the most for their money.

Whereas a single man regards his automobile as a part of his courtship and mating pattern, a single woman does not. To her an automobile is necessary for her transportation to and from her work, or it is an extension of her recreational life.

The car-buying pattern of married couples will follow the general pattern of their marital relationship. If the wife is dominating and forceful, she will control the selection of the family automobile. If the husband is the dominant person, he will do the deciding. For some married couples buying a car can be a traumatic experience. They may find themselves divided on questions of make, color, size, and cost. Their polarized positions may result in bitterness and strife. In a happy, loving relationship the couple will plan this new acquisition together, taking into account their individual preferences, their needs, and their financial ability.

PERSONALITY CLUES AND YOUR AUTOMOBILE

When you go to buy a car, you are doing more than purchasing a means of transportation. You are fulfilling a dream. You are answering a wish. You are also revealing your personality. The individual who selects a popular, medium-size, medium-priced car is saying, "Don't notice me, I'm just like everybody else." Such people don't want to be conspicuous but to blend into the herd. And they don't have to worry about criticism from others regarding their choice. After all, it's a choice many other people have made. These people are not certain of their own taste or judgment. By purchasing a car that is acceptable to so many they are sure that they must be doing the right thing. This blandness is further revealed in the quiet colors and upholstery they select. Their cars are never decorated with fancy gadgets. To them, being practical means being colorless and noncreative, and their automobiles usually reflect their sober devotion to leading the lives of ordinary citizens.

What about the man or woman who always purchases the latest new car? This is the owner who, was the first in his neighborhood to own an Edsel, a Comet, a Mustang, or a Maverick. Now he has or wants a Vega, Pinto, or Gremlin. The price, the style, the automotive features, don't really matter to him. He is an innovator. He is adventuresome. In temperament he is allied to the early explorers who sought out new, uncharted territory. These same individuals also rush to try out new tires, gasolines, and other automotive products. They don't have any special loyalty toward their automobiles, for they are more interested in the novelty and newness. It is being first that is important to them.

The convertible has a special significance for most people. Not only is it a sex symbol, but it signifies freedom, lack of restraint, and a "fun" attitude toward life. A woman patient who was depressed and felt inhibited and unloved by her family bought a convertible because it gave her the feeling of freedom she needed. To others the convertible can be an expression of bisexuality. In envy of women men may wish to have an opening of their own. The convertible satisfies that unconscious wish. A patient who was envious of his pregnant wife and her ability to have a baby bought himself a convertible—it satisfied his desire to have an opening from which a person could emerge.

Although these meanings may seem to have a bizarre touch, they are based on actual clinical material, taken from various patient analyses.

Volkswagen buyers are a special group. When you buy a Volkswagen, you don't just get a car; you also acquire a lot of friends—other Volkswagen owners. The Volkswagen is a way of life. More than that, it is a declaration of a certain attitude toward life and society. The Volkswagen owner is saying that he is concerned about economics, air pollution, and good craftsmanship. Volkswagen owners include students, professional people, and executives as well as a large number of older retired persons who appreciate economy and ease of handling. Creativity marks the Volkswagen owners. They usually take an intellectual and rational view of life. They are individualists. A Volkswagen owner is almost fiercely loyal to his "bug" and does not harbor secret wishes to own a Cadillac, a Thunderbird, or a Continental.

The growth of the suburbs has been responsible for a new concept in automobiles—the station wagon. The station wagon typifies comfortable living, away from the rush and noise of the city. In general, station-wagon owners are gregarious; they have a helpful attitude toward others. They are outwardly oriented, fond of people and animals. They have a social conscience and are usually active in political and civic affairs, particularly on the local level.

Running a close second in popularity for that suburban or small-town automobile is the sturdy four-wheel-drive vehicle. Owners of these are outdoor persons who can't wait to get away from it all. They may have a nine-to-five job in the city, but their hearts are in the wilderness. The owner of one of these cars is a rugged and independent individualist. He has great confidence in his own abilities. His idea of a good time is to go camping in some remote area. Manufacturers of these metal escape machines exploit the wilderness theme by giving them such names as Bronco, Scout, Land Cruiser, Land Rover, and Wagoneer.

THE BIG-CAR SYNDROME

In American cars there is a caste system that runs the spectrum from Continental and Cadillac down to the modest, stripped-down economy car. For many years the manufacturers of big cars have conducted advertising campaigns that have stressed the success image of those cars, their prestige and snob appeal. Their owners may know about and appreciate the qualities of their engines, but the average person who yearns for one doesn't care about the mechanical details. He is suffering from the big-car syndrome, which is widespread in this country.

What does the ownership of one of these cars reveal about the personality? Actually we would have to divide big-car owners into two classes. First, those who can afford big cars, and second, those who can't. In the first group the purchase of a big car may indicate ultraconservatism, a desire to retain the status quo of the social and political structure. The owner is not ashamed of either his money or his position and more or less takes it for granted. He feels that he is entitled to a big car, and he is going to enjoy it. It is also true that this owner may suffer from a social blindness that keeps him from seeing the slums as he drives past them. The colors of the big cars owned by persons in this group will probably be dark. The interiors will be sumptuous but not gaudy.

The second group of big-car owners are those who are out of their financial and social class. These people have the attitude of gamblers. It's an "easy come, easy go" world for them. They like to be objects of attention. They select flashy colors and the latest gadgets and other equipment. This owner of a big car may have to dine on hot dogs while his car consumes gallons of gasoline. He is happy, though, for even if his pockets are nearly empty, the big car he owns symbolizes to him a world of money, easy comfort, and no worries. Frequently, however, the big-car owner is unsure of himself and concerned about what other people think of him. He needs the ego boost that the big car gives him. He needs a dramatic symbol of worth to insure his place in society. Some big-car owners, however, have a secret admiration for the little car—particularly when they consider such matters as maintenance, gas mileage, and parking.

AUTOMOBILE ACCESSORIES AND PERSONALITY

For many people, selecting and buying an automobile is only one side of the coin. The other side is buying automobile accessories. Dressing up the car may be a substitute for adorning oneself. If you have trouble in personal grooming, you may put all that effort into grooming your car. You are unable to dress up yourself because you have a defective self-image. You see yourself as poorly groomed and sloppy. Since you are willing to accept this self-image, you do not attempt to improve yourself but instead improve your car's appearance. At the local post office I frequently meet a man who is unshaven and wearing wrinkled clothes. His automobile, however, is always washed and waxed. He doesn't wear a tie, but his car has all the latest accessories, including wire wheels. What he is saying in effect is "Don't look at me, I'm a slob. Look at my car."

Automobile accessories also satisfy our childish and adolescent desires for gadgets and playthings. It is socially acceptable to satisfy these urges by buying various devices and insignias for your automobile. Another reason for the purchase of automobile accessories is that in this age of mass production when each unit looks like the other, many people feel the need of distinguishing their personal items. This is particularly true with automobiles. Since the automobile is an extension of self, of personality, one does not want anonymity for it. Just as you don't want to look like another person, you don't want your car to be taken for one belonging to another person. You think *you* are unique, and you want your automobile to be unique also. For this reason you may customize your car with decals, flowers, signs, bumper stickers, rally stripes. Or you may dress up the inside with seat covers, floor mats, compasses, and decals. A popular decal reads, "This automobile specially made for _____." Owners of these personalized signs gain a certain emotional satisfaction from them. They know it is not true, but it is an expression of a wish.

Men who have fantasies of themselves as pilots or race drivers are usually discontented with the ordinary automobile instrument panel. They will add a compass, an ammeter, a tachometer, and other gauges. All of these help to preserve the illusion that the driver is not just an ordinary driver riding down the highway. He is a pilot, a navigator, a sensitive mechanic. This driver may be so busy watching his dials and listening for engine noises that he does not see the countryside through which he drives.

Adornment may also be combined with superstition or religion. Statues of the Virgin, St. Christopher, and other saints are popular. Stuffed animals are placed in the rear deck carrying out the teddy-bear motif of childhood. A good-luck symbol such as a pair of baby shoes or a rabbit's foot may dangle from the rearview mirror. All these things also satisfy our latent exhibitionistic impulses.

AUTOMOBILE ACCIDENTS AND PERSONALITY

To some individuals, driving an automobile is game, not necessarily of skill but of speed. Automobile accidents occur with frightening regularity, yet they do not frighten most people into better, more careful driving habits. Most drivers take the it-can't-happen-to-me position. And when it does happen to them, they are bewildered and angry. Because most people regard their automobiles as an integral part of themselves, they feel pain and anguish when their cars are struck. This is particularly true when the accident is not their fault. A driver who comes out to find that his car has been damaged in a parking lot experiences emotional pain. Women in particular are upset by this type of an accident, which can be partly traced back to rape fantasies. It is not uncommon for girls at the age of puberty to have such rape fantasies. As they grow older, these fantasies become repressed, only to emerge later in a crisis situation such as an automobile accident. This is particularly true for hit-and-run accidents.

Men who overreact to accidents are men who strongly identify with their automobiles in a sexual way. A crumpled fender affects them as if they had been castrated. A man who behaves in this fashion has an excess of castration anxiety.

Any driver, however skillful and careful can be involved in an accident, but some drivers regularly drive carelessly. They are accident-prone drivers. One type is the reckless driver who likes to play Russian roulette with his automobile. Sometimes this individual has a counterphobic attitude—that is, he attempts to repress a fear by deliberately courting the fear. He may be afraid, but he attempts to conceal it by driving in a reckless way, playing "chicken" with his car in an attempt to prove that he is not afraid of death. This is a favorite game among young hot rodders who are intent upon proving their manhood and courage if only in this negative way.

Another accident-prone driver is one who has self-destructive tendencies. He may have strong suicidal feelings that cause him to take chances and drive carelessly. He is constantly getting into minor accidents and banging up his car. Characteristically, he is so wrapped up in his own unhappiness that he does not consider the welfare and safety of other people.

YOU AND YOUR AUTOMOBILE

What is the place of your automobile in your life? Are you married to your car? Does your family place second to your automobile in your affections? Do you neglect them or your friends to fuss over your car?

A couple who had marital trouble came for counseling.

"He cares more for the car than for me," sobbed the wife. "He's always fussing around with it. Why, when I get sick, he's not concerned, but you should see how he carries on if there's a scratch on the car."

She was right. Her husband did spend more time and energy on the car. On Sundays, instead of spending time with his wife, he washed and polished the car. Although he was rarely affectionate or loving with her, he would pat the car fondly. He did not bring presents to his wife, but he continually purchased new things for the car.

"I needed a new winter coat," his wife complained bitterly, "but after he bought new tires, there wasn't any money left for my coat!"

Another patient suffered from varying degrees of depression when his wife left him and obtained a divorce and his business interests declined. His most severe attack of depression, though, came when his car was repossessed. He found that he had become sexually impotent. Losing his car was a kind of emasculation for him.

Air pollution problems may cause technical and mechanical modifications to be made in automobiles, and restrictions may be placed on when and where they may be driven, but the automobile as a symbol of aggression and sexual power will only be challenged when our society itself and our social structure are changed.

2

"I've Got the Meanest Dog
on the Block!"

EXPRESSING PERSONALITY TRAITS THROUGH PETS

As soon as men learned to shape their environment and developed the necessary skills for survival, they began to feel cravings for adulation and obedience, and the first pet was domesticated. Man found that he could be master over another living creature and that that creature would show him the affection and respect he felt he deserved and could not always be sure of getting from his fellow humans.

Since then, men have used pets to express desires of various kinds and in the process revealed much about their personality traits. A pet becomes a mirror in which personality is revealed, sometimes even characteristics that have been repressed or successfully hidden from other people.

Attitudes toward animals in general, including those in the zoo, are also revealing. You may project onto animals some of your own repressed emotional feelings. Often, too, your responses toward animals, especially pets, indicate your true attitudes toward other people. The psychology of pet ownership and attitudes toward animals is really the psychology of personality adjustment. Some of the psychological tangles in pet ownership become even more interesting when you consider some of the meanings of the word "pet." "Pet" is a base word with a double meaning. The double meaning is also a meaning of opposites. Such a word is very interesting to psychiatrists because it indicates a prime word that comes from the depths of the unconscious. It is therefore a word that has profound significance. The word "pet" means a loved and cherished creature, idea, or object. It also means to stroke or caress. It *also* means a fit of peevishness or ill temper. Thus we have positive libidinal feelings on one side and aggressive, destructive ones on the other side. Case histories show that much of the behavior of people toward their pets reflects that double meaning.

People have a tendency to select pets that either look like them or reflect some aspect of their personalities, although this is usually an entirely unconscious process. Nervous people end up with nervous pets, and calm people have calm animals. Busy, talkative individuals will have busy, yapping dogs such as terriers, Chihuahuas, Pekingese, or Pomeranians, or they may have Siamese cats. The slow, lethargic individual will prefer a sheep dog, a basset hound, or some other kind of pet such as goldfish. It is also true that the owner's temperament will sometimes affect his pet's emotional traits.

The hypochrondriac extends his concern about his health to include his pet's health. He not only takes pills for his imaginary ills but also gives them to his pet. There is now a complete line of animal medicines, which includes vitamin pills, tranquilizers, laxatives, antibiotics, aspirin, digestive aids, and cough syrups. The next time you give your pet a pill, stop and think: Are you treating your pet or yourself?

Often people will project their own neuroses and fears onto their pet animals. It is amusing and transparent when four-year-old Johnny explains his reluctance to go to sleep in a dark room because the dark frightens his puppy. We know that he is projecting his own fears onto his pet. It is not always so obvious when adults do the same thing. Mrs. X. is afraid of flying, but she doesn't like to admit to it. Instead, she says that flying upsets her pet poodle, so she travels by automobile or train with him. No one can accuse her of being a coward, Mrs. X. thinks. Instead, she expects to be praised for being so considerate of her pet's feelings.

Impulses that may be suppressed are sometimes projected onto pets. Thus, the man who has a repressed desire to bite people will encourage his dog to bite people. He has not been able to progress emotionally from the childish oral sadistic state, but he has learned to control his impulses. If he feels sufficient social pressure to keep his dog from biting people, he may encourage the dog to simulate biting by playing roughly with him.

Carl was a typical oral character; though an adult, he was still in the oral stage of emotional development. Characteristically, he had never married but still lived at home with his parents. A large obese man, Carl looked like an overgrown child with his slightly pouty expression. All his pleasures were oral: He ate large meals, and between meals he snacked, and when he wasn't eating, he was chewing gum or smoking. His pet dog, a Doberman pinscher, was fat from being overfed. The dog was also mean and liked to nip at people's heels.

Just as oral impulses are revealed through pets, so are anal tendencies. The individual whose personality and emotional development is still in the anal stage may be an adult who still resents his toilet training. In reality he is in rebellion against the imposition of that training. As an adult he can express that rebellion through his dog—which he does by permitting the dog to defecate on the neighbor's lawn or in the middle of the sidewalk. In more extreme cases of conflict over toilet training he may permit the dog to have "accidents" in the house or in or near stores or other dwellings. This attitude may include feelings of contempt for other people, especially for persons in authority. The dog or other pet is permitted to do what the individual would like to do without the fear of a reprimand from society or from a parent-figure.

Having a large dog gives some people a sense of superiority. It falls in the same category as having a car with more horsepower, having a bigger color television set, or going to Europe while your neighbors go to a nearby resort. As an exercise in social snobbery it says several things. It shows that you can afford the expense of feeding a big dog, that you have the space in which to keep such a dog, and that you are of such importance personally and have such an abundance of material possessions that you need to be protected from the rapacity of those less fortunate. It may be one way of advertising yourself and displaying your own estimate of your worth and importance.

It has been observed that some people who are kind to animals are disagreeable to people. Mary, for example, was very intolerant of other people and their actions. She was critical and sarcastic, refusing to excuse mistakes even when they were unintentional. Her pet dog, however, was always excused no matter how he behaved. When he did something destructive, she said he was "just playful," and when he wet on the rug, she said he was "nervous." Mary could excuse animal misbehavior but not human mistakes. Her personality was a rigid antisocial one, yet she expected to be praised for her "kindness" toward animals.

Reaction-formation is also shown by attitudes and relationships toward pets. This, in psychoanalysis, is the development of socially acceptable attitudes which are actually in opposition to repressed impulses or desires. Thus, an adult may be so ashamed of a childhood attitude that he assumes the opposite attitude as an adult. He may feel so guilty over some childhood act that he spends a lifetime trying to do penance for that act. It is an interesting psychological fact that many people who become very active in animal protection and rescue societies are actually concealing a past inclination toward animal cruelty. This may even have included acts of animal mistreatment. Now because of guilt, they transfer those feelings into acceptable rescue fantasies and pursue various humane activities.

AGGRESSION, AUTHORITY, AND ANIMALS

George Eliot concisely stated one reason pets are so popular when she said, "Animals are such agreeable friends. They ask no questions, they pass no criticisms." It is also true that animals may provide a natural outlet for aggressive impulses, and although most pet-owners seem to be letting their pets run their lives, others have pets so they can be aggressive and authoritarian toward them. Is that your attitude toward you pets? Do you enjoy the natural dominion you have over them? You may be one who takes to heart the biblical injunction to "have dominion over the fish of the sea, and over the fowl of the air, and over every living thing that moveth upon the earth."

If you like having an animal dependent upon you, it shows that you enjoy being master in a master-slave relationship. Since such a relationship is difficult if not impossible to establish on the human level, you indulge yourself by playing God to a fawning dog. The tyranny you cannot always establish over your family you can establish over your pets.

"Give me my dogs anytime," Mr. Y. said in disgust as he talked about his teen-age sons. "My dogs stay in at night. They jump when I whistle. They obey my commands. They take baths when I decide they should. They're glad to see me when I come home. They seem to understand me."

Mr. Y. was making the common mistake of comparing trained, disciplined dogs to young, normally rebellious boys. What he refused to see was that he had always had a better relationship with his dogs than with his sons.

"If he had spent as much time with the boys and trained them as well, our lives would all be happier today," his wife said bitterly.

One man who hates his lowly position in a large office acts the part of "boss" with his pet animals. Another establishes his dominion over his pet dog by making the animal eat the same health foods that he eats.

Do you use your pet as a safety valve for your aggressive emotions? When you become irritated or angry and take out those feelings on your pet, you are revealing your lack of maturity—you are behaving like a child. Persons with strong sadistic impulses feel safe in being cruel to animals. Although there are laws against inhumane treatment of animals, there is too often little likelihood of its being discovered. Animals cannot go to relatives or neighbors and tell what has happened.

An unconscious sadistic impulse is often satisfied under the guise of discipline. "He just doesn't seem to learn unless I give him a good smack," explained one dog-owner when he was remonstrated by a friend for striking his dog. This explanation sounded reasonable until he was observed kicking the dog immediately after he discovered he had a flat tire on his automobile.

Parents should be concerned if they discover their youngsters consistently mistreating a pet animal. This could be indicative of serious emotional or mental illness. Children usually have to be taught about kindness to animals, but it should not be a lesson that has to be continually repeated. Mean children become mean adults.

Some sadistic children and adults like to tease zoo animals. They are bullies who would turn and run if facing a wild animal in the open, but they feel safe in tormenting the animals that are behind bars or protective moats. Some others satisfy their sadistic impulses by training dogs, where affection is replaced by aggression. Hunters who train and use dogs can satisfy all their sadistic and aggressive impulses in an approved way, and some take advantage of this socially acceptable activity by being physically or verbally abusive to the animals when away from any possible censure by other people. Some men even think it is proof of their masculinity to curse and kick at animals. Any person, no matter what age level, who exhibits evidence of cruelty toward animals needs professional help. He or she is a sick person.

A carefully repressed or sublimated hostility toward other people may be expressed in keeping a vicious dog.

"I've got the meanest dog on the block!" a man bragged to me and others at a party. I took a second look at him. He had spoken with such obvious pride! Why was this so important to him? Vicious pets, especially dogs, are kept by persons who feel insecure. They themselves may be small in stature and physically weak with a fear of physical danger. In other words, the little man hides behind his dog, at least emotionally and psychologically. In the case of the man at the party his problem became obvious when his wife joined our group. Not only did she outweigh him by many pounds, but she was also taller. She immediately dominated him and the other members of the social group. Within a ten-minute period she contradicted him no less than four times, and she interrupted him when he was talking. He didn't have a chance to express himself in conversation. It was through his dog that he was able to express his hostility.

He reminded me of a patient I had treated for anxiety symptoms. The symptoms had developed after his wife insisted that he get rid of his large ill-tempered dog. "Of course, the dog did bite her," he admitted, "but it was just an accident." But was it just an accident? Analysis revealed that he unconsciously wanted to hurt his wife because of her domination and nagging. He had fantasies and dreams in which he killed her. Too afraid and henpecked to assert himself and assume the role he coveted, he acquired a mean dog. He encouraged this dog to be aggressive toward other people. It was only a matter of time until the dog would bite someone. For this patient, having the dog injure his wife was psychologically acceptable. He disclaimed any responsibility for the act, and he refused to recognize the true significance of it.

In the wake of an increased crime rate watchdogs have acquired a new popularity. They protect property and lives and are particularly valuable around commercial and industrial sites. However, it is the attitude of the watchdog-owner that interests us. Many times the person who is in no real danger of being attacked or robbed will keep the most vicious watchdog. Keeping a vicious or aggressive dog is often a case of self-aggrandizement rather than self-protection. The possessor of a vicious dog, or sometimes just a very large dog, shows strong antisocial tendencies. You've put the world on notice with such a pet: "Watch out for me, or you'll get hurt." Another personality trait may also be revealed—a sense of insecurity. As a child you hung on to your mother's skirts; now you hang on to your dog's leash.

SEXUALITY AND PETS

Pets frequently have a sexual significance for their owners; like any other possession, pets can assume a phallic symbolism. Many times they actually represent the sexual attitudes of their owners, and in some cases they also supply a vicarious sex life for them.

Mr. B. suffered from impotency. He had a mongrel dog that he allowed to run loose, and although several neighbors complained, Mr. B. refused to confine the dog. He took pleasure in recounting the dog's sexual adventures and how a neighbor's pedigreed dog had become impregnated by his mongrel. Almost all Mr. B.'s sexual thrills were supplied secondhand through his dog. He was so involved in the borrowed personality of the dog that he experienced sexual excitement when he saw the dog copulating.

Mrs. E. has an unhappy marriage. She blames her husband, who is weak and unaggressive in business and at home. She has a pet cat, a tom who behaves in characteristic male-cat fashion. Although Mrs. E. would deny it, she actually gets pleasure from imagining the adventures and sexual life of her cat, whom she has named after a popular motion-picture star.

There is a strong urge toward exhibitionism in Mr. J.'s personality. It comes out in his choice of a pet dog. Mr. J. has a short-haired dog whose sex organ can be clearly seen. He admits that it gives him a thrill to see this. As a child Mr.

J. liked to go to the animal barn at the county fair to see the stallions and bulls. As an adult he always notices the sex organs on animals at the zoo. In this he is not unusual or abnormal, for watching animals in the zoo engaged in sexual play is a favorite pastime for many visitors. It is one reason monkeys are so popular, for while they resemble people in many ways, their lack of inhibitions, especially in sexual play, gives satisfaction to onlookers who on occasion would like to behave in similar ways.

Some adults report that their first sexual experiences were connected with childhood pets; this sometimes consisted of masturbating the animals or of being sexually aroused or stimulated by them. There are also cases of attempted or actual sexual intercourse with animals. Alfred Kinsey found that about 8 percent of the male population had had a sexual experience with an animal, most commonly boys reared on farms or ranches. Some sexually starved women have fantasies in which they engage in sexual intercourse with animals. Such acts are also present in mythology in such tales as Leda and the Swan and Europa and the Bull and when Zeus appears in animal form to abduct and rape girls. Some individuals who receive sexual thrills from watching animals engage in sexual intercourse may become animal-breeders. Sexual and sadistic feelings are often present at the same time. These feelings may account for individual acts of cruelty to pets as well as public events that involve animal cruelty such as bullfighting and cockfighting.

SELECTING A PET

The way you select or acquire pets indicates something about your personality and emotional attitudes. You may have a superficial reason for wanting a particular kind of pet when actually there is a hidden reason, one you may not even be aware exists. The man or woman who feels socially insecure may do one of two things. On the one hand, to hide his insecurity, he will purchase a pet of unquestionable pedigree—don't ask me about my family history, just look at my dog's ancestry. These people can get rid of their disappointment at not having royal ancestors by having dogs of impeccable breeding. Not for them the neighborhood foundlings! They buy their dogs at established kennels and pay large sums of money to secure a "good" dog. A woman who had recently acquired wealth but no social status spent several hundred dollars buying some pedigreed Abyssinian cats. It didn't give her an entrée into local social circles, but it did give her status among cat-owners.

Another reaction of the person who feels socially inferior may be to reinforce that feeling by selecting a nondescript or "mutt" dog, saying in effect, "Look, I'm worthless. Even my dog is no good!" How many times have you heard someone say of his pet, "Oh, he's nothing. He's just a mutt!" The unspoken implication is, "I'm nothing much either." These people will usually get their pet from the local animal shelter.

One particular breed of dog will often be "fashionable." Thus, at one period cocker spaniels were in style, later poodles, and recently Yorkshire terriers have been the "in" breed. If you select the currently popular breed of dog you are probably one who follows the leader. Your ambitions are modest, as are your home and automobile. You stick close to the center in your opinions. You prefer to let other people make decisions for you. Selecting the most fashionable dog may compensate for your own lack of fame.

If you select as a pet some unusual or exotic animal, you are trying to attract attention. You may feel you are insignificant as a person, but you know people will look at you if you walk around town with a leopard on a leash. A tiger in your car or a lion in your yard will guarantee you some headlines as well as complaints. You can borrow color for your personality from your unusual pets, but it's not very lasting. It has a way of fading when the excitement and shock wear off.

Do you have a special fondness for lost animals? This may be the outward expression of an inner fear. You may be saying to an unlistening world, "Look, I'm lost. Will somebody please stop and care!" You feel a sympathetic kinship with these lost animals. Persons who have recently suffered a personal loss in their lives will often go to the animal shelter and adopt a lost or abandoned animal, trying to fill a gap in their lives by taking on responsibility for another creature. Sometimes, too, they are so emotionally distraught over their loss that they turn to animals for comfort, feeling that they have been betrayed willingly or unwittingly by fellow humans.

How Pets Can Reveal Emotional Problems

In many cases pets can furnish clues to important, often repressed emotional problems. Most people, for example, relate kindness to animals with social awareness and emotional maturity. However, kindness to animals like any other character trait can be stretched to unreasonable and imprudent bounds. If your home and yard are overrun with pets, you have an emotional problem. You may be good-hearted, but you may also be improvident. Your inability to say No to a stray animal is probably only one area of your life in which you do not function effectively. The person who finds himself gradually inundated by dogs and/or cats is responsible for his predicament and will have to suffer the consequences. Mrs. A. had somehow managed to acquire thirteen dogs, three cats, and two goats, all in a five-year period. She suffered from tension and other feelings of anxiety. She no longer had any social life, for it took most of her energy and money to feed and care for her pets. Many of her friends had ceased to call on her. "It's too noisy and smelly," one of them said frankly. Her personal life was in confusion. She admitted that the housework was rarely finished. Letters were unwritten, books and papers were unread, and the checkbook was unbalanced.

The pets, however, were only one symptom of her emotional problems. Those problems had started when Mrs. A.'s husband left her. They were compounded when her parents died. Left alone, Mrs. A. found herself unable to cope with the myriad details of daily living. She used pet animals as both an excuse for falling behind in her work and an attempt to assuage her loneliness. Mrs. A. was persuaded to find homes for all but one cat and one dog. She moved to a smaller house, which she could care for properly and without too much effort. In addition, she was encouraged to join a church group, to do volunteer work, and to make herself and her time available to other people rather than exclusively to animals. The result was a new life, one in which she could function more easily.

How many pets do you have, and how did you get them? Do you really want and enjoy your pets, or are they excuses or substitutes for something you are trying to hide or forget? If you limit your social activities because you feel you should be home with your pets, what you are actually revealing is a tendency toward masochism. You have an emotional need for pain, a need to suffer indignities. A person who has allowed himself to be imposed upon by parents may substitute a pet animal when the parents are no longer available to impose on him.

Pets may also show your inability to relate well to other people. If you keep snakes for pets, you are not really a very friendly individual. I am not talking now about children who will keep almost any kind of a pet and love it and enjoy it nor about scientists or students of natural history, but about the ordinary person. I knew two people who collected snakes and made pets of them. One did it because he disliked people. "Folks don't stay around here long," he said gleefully, "and my relatives hardly ever come at all anymore." The other man admitted he got a thrill out of shocking people by handling snakes. For him it was a way of showing his superiority. He got satisfaction from being able to do something that other people couldn't or wouldn't do. To both of these men snakes were only means to an end. They were not objects of concern or love. This same attitude can be connected with other kinds of pets. Pets sometimes become pawns in family relationships. If you have a pet that you use as a lever in family arguments, you are not fond of the pet. You are using it. It is just a device for you to try to get what you want.

PETS AS PSEUDOPEOPLE

It has been said that a dog is man's best friend. Certainly the reverse seems to be true! This friendship may be good and valuable, but not if it is to the exclusion of human contacts and relationships. If you are trying to make a pseudo-human out of your pet, take a good look at your interpersonal relationships. Are they satisfactory? A disappointment in some area of human relationships often turns people away from other people and toward pets. They try to establish a meaningful relationship with a dog, a cat, a bird, or other pet. Yes, pets can alleviate loneliness, but they should not take the place of human companionship.

Most people try to humanize their pets. They ascribe to them human qualities, qualities that often reflect their own personalities. They endow their pets with human thoughts, desires, and plans. They insist that Fido is almost human in his reactions, and they see smiles, frowns, and other evidences of emotional reactions. "See, he's frowning," one woman said of her cat. She then spent nearly thirty minutes trying to discover what could be displeasing to her pet. Ascribing human motives and actions to your pet reveals an unwillingness to face reality.

Humanization of animals has become a billion-dollar business, one of whose most successful practitioners is the Walt Disney organization. Ever since Mickey Mouse, it has provided a steady series of animals with human characteristics whose appeal has been to adults as well as to children. Our affluent society has also been notorious in sharing its affluence with its pets. Dogs are the pets who get most of this special consideration. They have clothes to wear and fancy accessories, including jewelry, beds, dishes, blankets, and cosmetics. I recently saw an advertisement for cat beds. These beds included a four-poster style and bunk beds in case you had two cats. There is also a variety of houses for both cats and dogs. Some of these are quite elaborate and include carpeting, sun decks, and other "home comforts." There are even special birdcages, aquariums for your favorite fish, and furniture for pampered mice! Some owners take their pets for beauty treatments, rides, and trips. They may do without treats for themselves but never forget their pets.

What has caused all this pampering of pets? What does it show about our civilization, and what does it show about the pet-owner? Only in a society that has progressed from frontierism to foolishness would such a misplaced emphasis on luxury occur. Many pet-owners complain that their pets do not seem to appreciate these luxuries. They look on in dismay while their dogs take their ease on chairs and beds instead of in their dog beds. The owners feel betrayed when their pets refuse to accept the scientifically designed toys, the special food, and the "cute" clothes. It could be that some dogs and cats have more sense than their doting owners!

In some childless homes pets have an unnatural position of importance. Frequently they take the place of children to their owners and are treated like children, and they are so much a part of the family circle that a stranger hearing about them would not know that they were not real children. This emphasis on the pet as a child personality is not confined to married couples but is also found in the homes of unmarried people, where, too, it wrongly serves as a love substitute. It was difficult to be friends with Mr. and Mrs. T. as their acquaintances soon discovered. Cricket, a bulldog, was the main interest in this childless couple's lives, and they lavished all their parental concern and love upon the dog.

"Cricket is really a nice dog," one friend said, "but I feel like a fool sitting around listening and talking about him all evening. Besides, it spoils my appetite to have him sitting at the table just like a person!"

Another friend complained that her friendly relations with the T. family were strained when she didn't send Cricket a birthday card. "I can't always remember my grandchildren's birthdays," she said, "so why should they expect me to remember a dog's birthday!"

To some people the attitude of Mr. and Mrs. T. toward their dog is ridiculous and laughable. To others it is repugnant. In any case it is not an unusual attitude. For many people animals take the place of adult or child companionship. One of the reasons for the popularity of monkeys as domestic pets is their close resemblance to humans, especially human babies. They have hands, little bodies that can be cuddled, and an inquisitive interest in their surroundings.

A pet animal may be lovable, but it cannot give you back the love you really need as a person. A pet may be clever in learning tricks, but it can't communicate with you as another person can. The pet-owner relationship is a static one-sided one. If you insist on including your pet in all your social activities, you are actually exhibiting antisocial feelings toward other ꞌpeople. "Love me, love my dog" is not the statement of the well-adjusted, emotionally mature individual.

PARENTS, CHILDREN, AND PETS

Children correctly judge your attitude as a parent by the way you treat the family pet. They seem to realize that this is a fairly accurate representation of how you feel toward them, especially how you unconsciously feel about their instinctual impulses, which in many ways are not too divorced from those of the less inhibited pets.

Sometimes a pet will take the place of an imaginary companion. It is entirely normal for a child to have such a companion. This playmate who becomes very real to the child serves an important function in his adjustment to life and to other people. He is able to express his emotions, wants, and needs and gain some psychological satisfaction from this unseen friend. When a pet fills this role, it becomes more than an animal, a bird, or other creature. It acquires and assumes a complete personality. The pet becomes the alter ego of the child. It becomes all the things that the child wishes to become. It may have the personality of a warrior or an explorer. In this way a child may fulfill his desires and relieve some of his frustrations. There may therefore be serious emotional problems if the pet becomes sick, dies, or disappears. The child sees and feels a threat to his own personality when this happens. The imaginary companion is a transitional stage in children. It is a developmental stage that is very important in the formation of characteristics of imagination, creativity, and social adjustment. Pets can play a vital part in this period of a child's life.

Many times parents will direct criticism at and punish pet animals instead of criticizing or punishing the children. This is especially true if the pets happen to be important to the children. A child becomes frightened when his loved pet is threatened in any way or when he feels that there is a possibility of having his pet taken away from him. This, incidentally, can be any kind of pet. A pet turtle is as important to one child as a pet dog is to another. It is not the size or kind of animal but the intensity of the child's feeling toward it. The child wants you to treat his pet as well as you treat him, for to him the pet is a real personality with feelings similar to his own.

Taking away a child's favorite pet can have serious and deep effects upon his future emotional life. If you, as a parent, try to punish your child through his pet, you are displaying emotional immaturity and pettiness. You are also revealing cowardice. You are afraid to assert yourself as a parent and punish your child directly. To scold the child or even temporarily banish him is to risk losing his love. But discipline demands punishment, so you punish his pet.

Jealousy may be involved in your attitude toward family pets. "That kid thinks more of his dog than of me," a father complained. He would have been indignant if he had been told that he was suffering from jealousy. But he subsequently confirmed this hidden feeling (by his action) when he "accidentally" ran over the dog with his automobile.

Your attitude as a parent toward your child and his pet may have an effect on his ability to adjust to adulthood and to solve problems in adult living. Bill came to me because he was suffering from excruciating leg pains. No organic cause could be found for his malady, but he was unable to work because his legs were giving him so much trouble. In the course of his analysis a long-repressed memory came back to him.

"When I was about eleven years old," he said, "I had a pet dog, a boxer. We were great pals. I loved him more than anybody. I guess I didn't know too much about training him. He used to steal food from our kitchen. It would make my mother furious. One day he took our supper meat. My father saw him and hit him with a wrench he had in his hand. It broke his leg, and he had to be put to sleep. I remember I cried for days."

This memory was the clue to Bill's leg pains. He had his own apartment now and a pet dog. He had recently become engaged. Unfortunately, his fiancée did not like dogs. The possibility of having to give up his dog brought back the old traumatic memory, but with the pain transferred to himself. Bill was more emotionally attached to his pet than to his girl. When he broke his engagement, his leg pains disappeared. Later he met and married a girl who shared his liking for dogs.

Bill was able to make a satisfactory adjustment in his life to accommodate his special feelings toward his dog, and fortunately he was able to later make a suitable personal contact with another person. But some people are never able to make their lives meaningful in terms of interpersonal relations. They devote themselves to their pets, sacrificing all other aspects of their lives.

PET-HATERS

Love for pets is the major part of the pet story, but there is another side—the pet-haters. Some people are absolutely repulsed by pets. They may even refuse to visit in homes where pets are kept. Antipet people are in the minority and are therefore sometimes silent about their feelings. But they may feel as strongly about not having pets as pet-lovers feel about having them. Several things about your personality can be revealed by your refusal to keep a pet. I am not talking now about the person who does not have a pet because he is not in the right circumstance—if you do not have a pet because you are living in an apartment house where pets are forbidden but you wish you had one, you are an animal-lover. But if you will not have a pet at any time and under any circumstances, you are a non-pet person.

Fear is sometimes the cause for your feelings, especially where dogs or cats are concerned. This fear may come from a traumatic childhood experience. It may reflect the fearful attitude of parents and other adults.

"I don't like dogs," one man said. "My folks would never let us keep a dog after one of our playmates was bitten by a dog. As a child I was frightened by the stories I heard about the suffering and pain from animal bites. I associated dog bites with death."

"I can't stand cats," another man said. "One jumped on me once when I was just a little kid. It really scared me. I've never forgotten it!"

Childhood fears and fantasies about animals are directly connected with their feelings and fears of their parents. Cats are associated with the mother, and dogs with the father. A child who fears that a cat will scratch or hurt him can be interpreted in terms of feeling that the mother does not love him. There is the fear that she may hurt him because she hates him. The child who is afraid of being attacked by a dog is expressing a disguised fear of his father. Animal symbolism in this way often appears in dreams in both childhood and adulthood. In the common dream of being chased by a large dog the dog represents the father who is going to punish the dreamer for something he has done.

Fear of disease caused by erroneous tales keeps some people from having pets. "My grandmother said dogs were filthy and caused sickness," one woman told me. "I really know better now, but I just can't bring myself to have a dog in the house!" Some people subconsciously bury these feelings by developing allergies to animals. This provides them with an acceptable excuse for not having a pet and assures them a certain amount of sympathy from other people.

People who dislike pet animals are frequently fearful of losing their self-control. To them animals represent the animal impulses within themselves which they cannot accept. These impulses are their oral, anal, and phallic impulses which they project onto the cat or dog. Seeing the uninhibited behavior of pets, a behavior they secretly envy, makes them tense and anxious. What these individuals are saying is, "I can't, so why should they?" Guilt may also be present in the feeling of such an antipet person. He is aware of his true desires, and he wishes to be permissive in his behavior but knows he can't be. He really envies animals their freedom of expression and action.

Another personality trait that may be found in antipet persons is fear of competition. They don't want to share the limelight with anyone, particularly not with an animal.

"Why don't you like dogs?" I asked Mrs. D. after she had delivered a long tirade against pets.

"They're so noisy," she said, "always yapping!"

Mrs. D. herself was a compulsive talker who monopolized every conversation. Naturally, she did not want to be interrupted by a dog.

Some husbands or wives resent pets if they feel that the pets take up too much of their marriage partner's time and attention. "My wife is more interested in the dog than in me!" Mr. R. complained. "She fusses over the dog all the time. She buys him special food. She has time to take him out for a walk, but she doesn't have any time for me." Mr. R. admitted that he had gotten the dog to keep his wife company when he had a temporary job overseas for his company. Mrs. R., as so many lonely wives do, had learned to lavish her attention and affection on a pet. She had perhaps discovered that in some ways a pet was more reliable—at least, it would not go off and leave her.

Fear of loss may keep you from having a pet, particularly if you have had a bad emotional experience in connection with a previous loss. "I won't have a pet," a neighbor told me. "I used to always have dogs, but when anything happens to them, I get too upset." The death of a favorite pet animal may cause severe emotional shock to its owner. This is particularly true if the animal meets a violent death. Frequently when this happens, the owner will refuse to have another pet. He may even refuse to talk about pets in general or see other people's pets. "I was heartbroken when my dog was poisoned," a woman told me. "I decided that as long as this world remained such a wicked place, I would never have another dog or any kind of a pet animal!" There are emotional risks in owning a pet, yes, but there are always emotional risks in living.

Stuffed toy animals are becoming increasingly popular in modern life and not just for children but for adults. The insecurity and tensions of today's living have contributed to a growing sense of alienation and frustration, and stuffed animals help to relieve those feelings. Millions of them are sold each year, many for the waiting arms of teen-agers or adults. Some lonely women cuddle child-sized teddy bears or other stuffed animals for a needed sense of satisfaction. It is childish, but for them it is better than empty arms. Stuffed toys are satisfactory pet substitutes for some individuals because they don't want to bother with feeding and caring for a live pet. A stuffed animal is not only no trouble, it gives no trouble. It is the ultimate in obedience.

Cuddling stuffed animals is a form of fetishism —a displacement of affection where substitute objects take the place of people. It is natural for children to turn to stuffed animals or dolls. The same tendency in adults is indicative of the isolation, increased mechanization, and growing impersonality of the world.

Looking at your pets is really just one way of looking at yourself, since any type of personality trait and any kind of fantasy can be displaced and projected onto your pets. Pets are useful in some cases such as when they are watchdogs, and they can be fun and a lot of company, especially for the person living alone. The way in which you treat your pet shows the slant of your personality, and if you treat it like another person, you are not being fair to yourself, to the pet, or to other people. Pets are not people, and it is wrong to attempt to treat them as people. Dress up a dog, and you have only made a monkey of yourself! Treating pets as people robs them of their own special animal qualities and robs you of your necessity to learn to adjust to other people. If your love for animals is merely a rejection of your fellow human beings, you are denying yourself your chance to develop a mature personality. Loving pets and being able to accept them as pets indicates emotional stability and a high level of self-esteem.

3

"Let's Shake on That"

MANNERS AND CUSTOMS

We can probably assume that manners first became important shortly after man's early attempts at tribal unity. Manners are the prevailing customs and ways of living of a people or a class of people. In an individual sense manners are the way one person treats another person.

It has become common to think of manners as only etiquette, but manners encompass much more. Manners include many kinds of behavior patterns, whereas etiquette is a prescribed form of conduct related to a specific situation, social occasion, or some form of special ceremony. Manners are dependent upon group culture, and what is suitable in one society may be totally unacceptable in another social group. An example of this is the practice of belching. In some cultural groups this is not only permissible but mandatory; in our own culture it is considered bad manners and offensive behavior.

MANNERS AND MASCULINITY

There exists a mistaken idea that manners are more important for women than for men. Wrong-headed ideas about what constitutes masculinity cause some men to adopt deliberate attitudes of rudeness. There is nothing appealing, however, about a man who is loud, brusque, unsympathetic, cruel, or domineering. These are not masculine qualities; they are brutish ones. Manners and masculinity go together. Parents who equate good manners with "sissy" behavior are in large part responsible for this male attitude toward manners. A boy who grows up thinking that rudeness is "manly" will have placed an unnecessary obstacle between himself and other people.

Children of either sex learn manners at home. If they have only the example of bad manners, they will grow up ill equipped to function effectively in a socially integrated situation. Children are natural copycats who tend to imitate the adults or others with whom they identify; thus, you can have a whole family who are well mannered, or you can have a family who chew with their mouths open, a family whose general conduct is one of rudeness, or a family of nose-pickers.

Your manners, perhaps more than anything else, reveal your true character. They mirror your personality. It is not what you say that impresses people the most; it is what you do and how you do what you do. Your manners—or your lack of manners—reveal the real you.

MANNERS AND CHARACTER

More than just "Please" and "Thank you," manners are the sum total of your outward responses: words, gestures, eating habits, and actions. The subject of manners appears frequently in literature and philosophy. The ancient Greek poet Menander said, "Manner not gold is woman's best adornment." Centuries later, William of Wykeham, a fourteenth-century English educator and clergyman wrote, "Manners maketh man." Ralph Waldo Emerson characterized manners as "the happy ways of doing things." However, one of the best descriptions of the importance of manners in relation to personality is found in Edmund Spenser's sixteenth-century work *The Faerie Queene,* in which appear these words:

> The gentle mind by gentle deeds is known
> For a man by nothing is so well bewrayed,
> As by his manners.

What do your manners "bewray"—that is, reveal—about you? Do they show you as a well-adjusted, emotionally healthy, and happy individual, or do they show you as a baby or a bore? The bore is a self-centered person who has insulated himself against awareness of other people and who ignores other people's wishes and interests.

I recall my uncle telling about a friend of his who bored everyone every time he opened his mouth. He not only talked incessantly but considered himself an expert on all topics. He interrupted other people and dominated conversations by sheer volume until his wearied listeners would gradually drift away. On one occasion he was telling my uncle and some others for the nth time about his trip to India and how fascinating he had found that country. "I tell you," he said, "some of those fakirs can toss a rope into the air, climb up the rope, and completely disappear. Can you believe that?"

"Oh, yes," exclaimed one bored listener, "and by any chance can you do the trick yourself?" But the hint was lost, for the bore never comprehends what he is doing to other people.

Some ill-mannered people have never grown up. If you insist on having your own way and throw an adult temper tantrum when you don't get it, you are behaving like a baby. When you sulk, create tension, or become irritable when you cannot have what you want; when you blame other people for things that are your own fault or are really no one's fault; then you are unreasonable and refuse to listen to logic, your childish attitude is giving you away. In a sense you're standing there with a lollipop in your mouth.

AGGRESSION AND MANNERS

Aggression is an id drive. As mentioned previously, the id is one of the three psychological divisions of the mind. As a part of your unconscious the id contains not only aggressive drives but sexual drives and repressed memories. The other divisions of the mind, the ego and the superego, also influence your thoughts, decisions, and actions.

To show you how the id, ego, and superego work in relation to manners, let's use this rather simple illustration. Picture this scene: You have been invited to a buffet supper by your boss, and you are eager to make a good impression. When you arrive at the party, you are not only nervous but hungry, and your hunger increases when there is a delay before the food is served. When at last you and the other guests are invited to the buffet table, your id says, "Push ahead of the others. You know how hungry you are. It isn't fair that you have been made to wait so long. Hurry, get all you want to eat before the others do and show them that you're not used to being kept waiting!"

Your superego, your center of training and morals, is horrified at this aggressive attitude and says, "Wait! You know you've been taught that it is rude to push ahead of others."

You now have a conflict in a manners situation, and it is time for your ego to step in and appraise the situation realistically: "If you want to make a good impression, you won't display bad manners by being pushy; besides, there is plenty of food for everyone." In this case the conflict is solved, and good manners win out; however, there are also many instances where aggression is the winner.

In social situations aggression usually shows up as rudeness—deliberate discourteous or impolite conduct expressed in words, gestures, and/or actions. Sometimes, too, you can display rudeness by what you don't say or by what you fail to do. When someone asks you a question and you have heard but do not answer, you are being rude. When you contradict others, you are being rude. In any social situation or interpersonal relationship there are hundreds of "contact" points when either rudeness or courtesy can be employed. The important thing about rudeness is that it is a deliberate act, an act of hostility toward others, an act of aggression no matter how one tries to justify it. When a secret agent takes on a false identity, his assumed characteristics and habits are known as his "cover." In the same way rudeness can serve as a cover for psychological problems. It can be an attempt to mask your inability to adjust successfully to other people or to hide the fact that you are unable to cope with reality. Rudeness or bad manners may be the outward indications of hidden depression, tension, fear, worries, or other anxieties. Sometimes bad manners are caused by physical pain. The reasons for rudeness vary with the individual and his psychological and emotional responses to life. In some individuals rudeness covers up a deep sense of insecurity. In others there is a false feeling of superiority. Youngsters sometimes feel it is "smart" to act rude; it is their weapon against adult authority and the adult world. A member of a minority group may be rude to express his anger against discrimination, and at the same time he himself may be a target of rudeness because many people feel safe being rude to a minority member of society. It is a way to work off their own irritations.

Frustration can also be revealed in your manners. It can produce a short temper which in turn produces bad manners.

"I'm sorry I was so rude the other day when you came by," a neighbor explained, "but I'd worked all morning trying to get the lawn mower fixed. I could have kicked it into the ditch!" Of course, he didn't kick it into the ditch (he was too sensible and thrifty to do that); instead, he verbally kicked the first unlucky person who happened to come by. Frustration can also come from feelings of insecurity and inferiority. You have a nagging feeling that you could be doing better than you are, or you may feel fearful because you aren't sure what to do. Thus, someone who is afraid that his ignorance or inadequacy will be revealed may deliberately adopt a pose of rudeness, hoping that by alienating people with his poor manners he can keep his inadequacies concealed. You may have met this person at your job—no one is sure whether or not he knows or is doing his job, since no one is brave enough to question him about it.

Shopping can and often does become an arena of aggression. Although slavery may be legally outlawed and morally frowned upon, the master-slave relationship still shows up in the clerk-customer confrontation. It is a situation in which poor manners are all too often prevalent, and in few other situations are individuals so tempted to behave rudely. Manners work both ways in stores. Clerks and other store personnel are obliged to exhibit good manners; customers, however, have no such obligation, and courtesy for them truly does reveal character. Many times persons who feel imposed upon in other areas of their lives will try to increase their feelings of importance by assuming an attitude of instant superiority over clerks. People who have built up a reservoir of aggression that they are afraid to release in the presence of those who know them will let it explode upon people who have to put up with their rudeness.

Recently I was in a store with an acquaintance and was shocked to hear how he berated the salesclerk when she failed to immediately produce the merchandise he wanted. He later defended his action by saying, "Well, I may have sounded cross, but after all she is here to serve people."

"But you don't treat your gardener or cleaning woman that way."

"No, when I get mad at them, I don't dare say anything. They're too independent. They'd both quit their jobs!"

It was saddening and also revealing to see that my acquaintance, a highly respected professional man, was really just a bully at heart.

Sometimes the worst manners are called forth by the act of driving. Men and women whose manners are normally faultless suddenly become rude and aggressive when they get behind the wheel. I have seen a driver honk his horn impatiently at a pedestrian crossing the street. The same man, if walking, would not think of brushing past another person on the sidewalk, but he has conditioned himself to be impervious to others once he is in his automobile. He uses it as a barrier betwen himself and other people.

Losing your manners when you consider it safe to do so because of the impersonality of the situation, as in the case of the driver, reveals a character defect. It is a way of expressing your contempt for people, a contempt that you conceal when you deal with people face to face. You are demonstrating antisocial feelings that actually indicate flaws in your own personality. Your inability or unwillingness to maintain the same level of good manners in all situations indicates an instability in your personality and the strong possibility of repressed emotional problems that only become noticeable in times of stress or when you feel safely anonymous. You are being insincere when you are polite to those who know you and impolite to those with whom you have only slight or no personal contact.

Being critical is also a form of bad manners. Angela prided herself on her manners and social graces, yet she was extremely critical of others. Like many people, she had developed a form of selective mental blindness, and she refused to see that being critical is just as rude as not saying "Thank you" or "Please." Angela would never have put out her foot and tripped anyone, but she thought nothing of tripping someone conversationally by criticizing him.

In all aspects of life there are areas in which you may be exposed to rudeness and areas in which you have the opportunity to be rude. It is a game in which you are sometimes a loser and sometimes an apparent winner, "apparent" because in rudeness you always lose psychologically and emotionally. Putting others down with rudeness is a way of putting yourself down. You are showing others that you not only don't care about them but don't care about giving a good impression of yourself. You have low self-esteem and are not concerned with how you appear to other people. By your rude manners you are exposing yourself as an unhappy, frustrated, and dissatisfied individual.

Good manners, on the other hand, show that you are a mature, well-adjusted person with sufficient self-esteem to be able to appreciate not only your own worth but the worth of other people.

MANNERS, MARRIAGE, AND THE FAMILY

Manners can make or break a marriage, and manners can mean a happy or an unhappy family life. Rudeness in marriage is a sign of extreme immaturity, a selfish response to life. This selfishness, if allowed to dominate your personality, can cause you to be unhappy, always disappointed in other people, and finally disappointed in life itself. Good manners, on the other hand, will help to build a happy marriage and family life; showing consideration and compassion for others adds to your own happiness and enjoyment of life.

"I never knew that my husband could be so polite and well mannered until I saw him at a recent sales convention," one woman told me. She went on to explain that at home her husband was surly and cross. "He never says 'Please' or 'Thank you,'" she said. "He doesn't show any consideration for me or the children."

"Have you talked to your husband about this?"

"Yes, several times, but he says he doesn't have to be polite at home if he doesn't feel like it. I know that he works hard, but does being relaxed have to mean having poor manners?"

No, I told her, relaxation is not synonymous with rudeness. Any marriage in which manners have been discarded is headed for serious trouble; at the very least it will mean unhappiness for the marriage partners.

If you have been guilty of leaving your best manners outside, try bringing them in. Treat your spouse and other family members just as you treat friends and strangers. You may be surprised at the difference good manners can make at home. Family members find it easier to communicate with each other, and the emotional and even the physical health of the family can be improved.

Interpreting Doodles

Doodles are like dreams in that they are a kind of unconscious activity, and as with dreams they may reveal hidden or repressed desires. They can also indicate your manners—if you doodle while someone is talking to you, you are showing them that you don't feel that they are entitled to your full attention.

Doodles have been used as an interview technique in emergency psychiatric interviews and have proved to be particularly helpful in interviewing patients who are unable or unwilling to talk but who will reveal their emotional problems in the drawings they make. When Charles Manson, accused slayer of actress Sharon Tate, was being tried, I was shown some doodles made by him, although I was not told who had done them. I saw clear signs of paranoid schizophrenia, signs of "magical" thinking, and other evidences of personality disorders.

Tom is at a sales meeting; not only is he bored but he doesn't like the sales manager who is conducting the meeting. As he sits there half listening but with an attentive look on his face, Tom is doodling. Thinking of the coming weekend, he draws a boat, a golf club, and a television set. When the sales manager announces that everybody will have to work on the coming Saturday, Tom's innocent doodles turn to more sinister items, and he draws a pistol and then a gallows with a hanging figure. He writes the initials of the sales manager and draws a line through them. In Tom's case doodling lets him work off his anger at the sales manager in a harmless way.

Lee, a bashful teen-ager, calls up a girl from school. He would like to ask her for a date but doesn't know what to say. As Lee talks to her about baseball and school affairs, he is doodling hearts on the pad by the telephone.

A patient I once had insisted that despite the evidence, he really had no serious marital problems. He spoke at length on how much he loved his wife and what a wonderful person she was and how happy their homelife had always been. Yet I had observed that he was consistently rude to his wife, and it was obvious that he hated her. On one occasion as we were discussing his home situation he began to doodle on a pad. As he began to talk about his wife, he drew a series of daggers. When I asked him about a recent incident in which he had run over his wife's pet dog, he drew a coffin, but there was a human figure in the coffin. When I pointed out to him the inconsistency of his words and his doodles, his anger erupted. He was then able to talk about his true feelings toward his wife and admit his dissatisfaction with his marriage.

Drawing a self-portrait will result in a fairly accurate representation of your self-image. In addition, it will show up some of your emotional and personality-adjustment problems. People who have doubts about their intellectual abilities will often draw self-portraits that show them with small heads. Persons who feel a burden of responsibilities will draw themselves as figures with broad shoulders and large hands. Women who have doubts about their physical attractiveness will show themselves as having large feet. Those with an uncertain sense of their femininity will neglect the eyebrows or eyelashes and fail to indicate breasts. The hair will be depicted in a straggly, unattractive way. People with dependent personalities may draw poorly depicted feet and legs which are not aligned with the body; there will be several buttons on the clothes of the figures. All these things suggest infantile tendencies. The person who draws such a self-portrait is saying, "Look, I can't stand on my own two feet. I need help, just as I did when I was a baby."

A person whose self-portrait features an absence of ears, round eyes with pinpoint pupils, and mutilated or incompletely formed hands is unable to become involved in the reality of his environment. This kind of person may be withdrawn and unable to have any form of sustained social commitments or intimate personal relationships.

Problems and fantasies related to sexual problems are also shown in self-portraits. Figures drawn with the hand in a pocket may indicate masturbation fantasies. There may also be an exaggeration of the sex organs. In cases of emotional problems related to sexual identification there may be a distortion of the secondary sex characteristics and sex organs or an absence of them. A patient who was being treated for anxiety attacks brought on by his fears of homosexuality revealed his sexual confusion by drawing a self-portrait in which he had a penis, breasts, and long hair.

Individuals who are low in self-esteem and have a lack of self-confidence find it difficult to draw self-portraits and usually fall back on drawing stick figures. In doing this they are indicating that they do not see themselves as three-dimensional personalities but as flat, lifeless figures.

Doodles are valuable because they give you a chance to work off steam as well as provide clues to the causes of your frustrations and troubled feelings.

TALKING WITH YOUR HANDS

Nervousness, restlessness, boredom, fear, and lack of self-confidence are all given away by your hands. You may go to an interview and speak calmly, but your hands will be used to express your actual state of nervous tension. You may play with a pencil, rub your fingers together, or play with papers and books. One man who had been interviewed for an important position told me, "I really didn't think I was uptight about this interview until I kept dropping things. My hands just couldn't seem to hang on to anything at all!"

Handshakes are one of the best indicators of personality characteristics and can be used to detect emotional feelings. Like doodling, they have been used as an aid in emergency psychiatric interviews. Originally, shaking hands was not the gesture of friendship that it is today; it was a gesture born out of fear and distrust. Back in the days when all men went armed with a sword or similar weapons there was always a crucial moment when strangers met. The question had to be quickly answered: Was this to be a peaceful meeting or a violent one? If peace was the intent, both men either laid down their weapons or did not draw them. They approached each other with outstretched, empty hands, and to further insure against possible trickery, each man took the right hand of the other to prevent him from changing his mind and drawing his weapon.

Today's handshakes are still used to disarm others but in a psychological sense. Bargains are sealed with a handshake, public figures are honored with handshakes, old and new friends are greeted with handshakes, and when we want to congratulate someone, we shake his hand.

Handshakes can be used to indicate sexual or romantic inclinations. A subtle squeeze when shaking hands may indicate a romantic interest. Tickling the palm of a girl or woman with the forefinger while shaking hands has always been considered a suggestive gesture implying sexual interest and an invitation to seduction. The person who is inwardly nervous but outwardly calm will give a clue to his hidden anxiety by having a moist palm when he shakes hands. Some individuals shake hands while simultaneously moving away; these people are chronically suspicious, and they may have paranoid ideas as well. Often they are looking for trouble in every situation, even a social one. The person whose handshake is limp usually has a limp personality. He gives the impression of having no bones in his hand; in his personal life he is indecisive. Colorless in his personality, he is easily overlooked in a social group and often suffers from depression because of supposed slights. Someone who barely shakes hands is afraid of contact. This may be directly related to sexual feelings. If this happens while shaking hands with a member of the same sex, it indicates a fear of latent homosexual impulses, but if it happens while shaking hands with a member of the opposite sex, it indicates a fear of heterosexual relations.

If someone shakes hands with you and at the same time pushes your hand back toward you, he is rejecting you. The person who is aggressive will squeeze your fingers in a viselike grip or pump your arm vigorously. He is trying to show you that he is master. A person with sadistic impulses may shake hands in such a way that it will cause you pain—squeezing or crushing your fingers or cutting into them with a heavy ring.

Gestures, posture, and facial expressions indicate personality traits and frequently emotional or personality problems as well. Broad gestures, smiles, and frowns are easy to interpret, but more subtle gestures and expressions require more perception. We are all familiar with such things as the clenched fist, used to signify defiance, anger, and other aggressive attitudes, and the pointed finger, used for emphasis and for accusation. Gestures that have become world-known and standardized are those for victory and peace. Some finger gestures have an obscene connotation. Some gestures of contempt reflect strong antisocial or antiestablishment attitudes. Belching and farting are also used to express contempt. People who scratch themselves while talking to others are demonstrating a "don't care" attitude toward social conventions. Lifting eyebrows, supercilious smiles, and vulgar gestures like thumbing the nose indicate contempt toward others.

Many persons who "talk" with their hands are insecure. They have doubts about what they are saying, so they try to cover up by creating a false atmosphere of excitement and urgency. These same people are usually very emotional and may be overtalkative and speak too loudly. Inferiority feelings are revealed by the person who tries to keep all gestures to a minimum; such a person is shy, introverted, and lacking in self-esteem. Depression is frequently indicated by a slumping posture, downcast eye, and an inability to face other people directly. Tenseness and apprehension are shown in a number of gestures. A man may run his hand through his hair or over the top of his head if he is bald; a man or woman may clasp the back of the neck. They are trying to tell themselves to relax. Distress is revealed by a constant preoccupation with one's physical appearance. The woman or man who fiddles with hair or keeps adjusting clothing is embarrassed and socially insecure. A woman may smooth out imaginary wrinkles or tug at her skirt, and a man may tug at his tie or finger his fly.

"Please don't hit me, I'm defenseless" is what the individual is saying who put his hands on top of his head. He fears punishment. Similarly, a folded-arms pose is a defensive and wary gesture. A woman patient always pursed her lips and became very tense whenever she was around a man. Analysis revealed that as a child she had been frequently slapped in the mouth by her father.

When they wish to get adult attention, young children will pull at an adult's sleeve or arm, tug at a coat or pants leg, or poke and jab at them. Most adults find this annoying and say so; it is even more annoying to have another adult pull at your sleeve or poke you to get your attention. The person who pokes you in the ribs or grabs at your sleeve or lapel is behaving childishly. He is immature with poor emotional adjustment and bad manners.

FOOD, EATING HABITS, AND PERSONALITY

Eating habits, food preferences, and attitudes toward food are personality indicators. Food plays an important role in the lives of most people beyond its obvious one as a necessity. There are many emotional and psychological facets to food and eating. At the very beginning of life being fed is the center and meaning of each day. Not only is nourishment gained in this way, but as the infant progresses in emotional knowledge, he learns that feeding time can also mean a time of cuddling by his mother and that if he refuses to eat, it can become a time of stress and anger. It is during this oral stage of development that many personality traits become firmly fixed and persist into adulthood. Oral orientation and satisfaction form the basis of our earliest adaptation to life and continue, therefore, to color our later emotional developments also. Eating habits and food itself become natural weapons in interpersonal contests and relationships. Children soon recognize this and will use food to get attention, to express anger, or to get what they want. A child learns at an early age that he can use food and eating as blackmail. He finds that by refusing to eat, playing with his food, or dawdling over meals he can upset his parents. They may even bribe him with toys and other rewards to make him eat better and faster.

Barney, a patient who was overweight, had

also been a fat baby and an overweight adolescent. He had been dominated to an excessive degree by his mother, who insisted he follow a rigid schedule and was strict in her habit training. His father would not let him learn to do things himself but would impatiently take over and finish what the boy had started. When Barney became an adult, his father still treated him as if he were incompetent. There was only one way in which Barney could assert himself and satisfy his need for independent action—through food. He became a compulsive eater. In other areas of his life Barney was controlled by others, but in eating he became master of the situation.

The fussy eater is really asking for attention. He often craves affection and has low self-esteem. In extreme cases of emotional disturbance the poor eater literally starves himself to death while trying to conceal an emotional problem or resentment. On the other hand some individuals who are starved for affection may turn to food for satisfaction. A woman whose husband was overweight sighed and complained about her mate's compulsive eating habits. It didn't require an expert, however, to notice that she never spoke affectionately of or to her husband. There were no spontaneous affectionate gestures or glances between them. Eating, munching, and nibbling had become love substitutes for the husband in his marriage.

Criticism of his wife's cooking is usually an expression of hostility by the husband. This hostility, although centered on food, actually encompasses their entire relationship. Food is a handy device on which to focus the built-up anger and unhappiness. Since his wife has spent her time and energy preparing the food, the husband by criticizing it is showing contempt toward her. Frequently such criticism starts a chain reaction which results in a series of arguments. Not only does dinner get cold, but so does love.

Juvenile attitudes toward food, eating, and table manners may be carried over into adulthood. Some people continue to snack between meals just as they did when they were growing up. Although they no longer need the extra food, they can't break the habit. Others continue to prefer the same foods they liked as adolescents—they will eat hot dogs or hamburgers, potato chips, ice cream, and french fries instead of a more adult-oriented meal. There is nothing wrong with these items as food except when they are a steady diet. Emotional factors are involved in the choice of these foods, which represent a time of less responsibility and may also represent an adolescent defiance of adult authority and an association with youthful ideas and feelings.

Wives who will not learn to cook or who are poor cooks are attempting to evade adult responsibilities. Playing house, not keeping house, is their subconscious desire.

Food faddists are often sex-starved people. They may have difficulty in relating on an emotional level with other people. Many times they are immature and have personality-adjustment problems. To compensate for their lack of love ties and sexual satisfaction, they turn to special foods and become preoccupied with their digestion and bowels. Buying these special foods keeps them busy, and being on a food-fad diet sets them apart from others, they think. In one sense these food faddists make pets of themselves, and therefore, the care and feeding of themselves becomes of prime importance.

Bad table manners are annoying to those who are forced to witness them, but this is often the subconscious wish of the offending individual; it is an expression of contempt and defiance. Thus, John is habitually late for meals. He does this purposely to annoy his wife. Although he may offer various excuses, this lateness is a deliberate expression of his hatred of his wife.

An adolescent may behave in an unmannerly way at the table to annoy his parents. He may come to the table unwashed, uncombed, and unkempt. He may eat his food noisily and slouch at the table. He may introduce topics of conversation that he knows in advance are going to be controversial and objectionable.

The individual who uses mealtime as a podium is a person who likes to dominate others. He wants to be the center of attention. The person who has sadistic impulses will use mealtime to quarrel, pick on others, or find fault. He doesn't want to let other people relax and enjoy a pleasant mealtime atmosphere. He recognizes that people are particularly vulnerable when they sit down to eat, for they do not expect to be attacked.

FOOD AS REWARD AND PUNISHMENT

Food has always been used as a reward-punishment device. Parents have traditionally punished children by sending them to bed without supper or withholding favorite foods, such as desserts. Good behavior, on the other hand, is often rewarded with a special food treat. Sometimes food is used as a bribe: "If you are good, you can have some candy." Food is also used in adult society for punishment and reward. We may not think of it in this way, but the implication is there. Prisoners may be put on short rations because of disobedience.

Adults, like children, may refuse to eat to punish other people. Harry quarrels with his wife and refuses to eat dinner. He is punishing her for the incident. Young Jane has a quarrel with her boyfriend. She breaks her engagement and retires to her room to cry. She refuses to eat. "I'm not hungry. I'll never eat again!" she states to her anxious parents. Of course, she'll eat again, at least in a day or two, but in the meantime she is punishing her boyfriend. People also punish themselves by not eating. They may claim to have allergies or digestive problems, but they really have emotional problems. If they have strong guilt feelings, they may feel that they are useless and unworthy. They act as their own prosecutors and jailers and withhold food from themselves.

"I can eat hardly anything," a woman patient complained. "I've stopped going out to eat, and I never accept dinner invitations anymore. Why go out when I can't eat the food?" Analysis revealed that she felt guilty over the way she had treated her aged parents. When they died, she developed a number of food allergies.

In adult life we continually use food as a reward. When we are happy, we enjoy a festive meal, and we celebrate special occasions by having a party with food and beverages. Dinners are given for employees who retire, for politicians who win, and for public figures who succeed. Annual company banquets, parties, and picnics are really bribes for good employee behavior. This is the philosophy of "Do your work well, don't cause trouble, and you can have a party."

An example of an ambiguous use of food in our society is the custom of the elaborate last meal for the condemned prisoner. Is that meal supposed to be a reward to the prisoner for accepting his fate, or is it a defense against our own guilt for executing the prisoner?

TIPPING

Tipping is a controversial subject, and in any group you are apt to find as many different opinions about it as there are people present. Tipping is part custom and part manners, and your attitude toward it can be very revealing about your personality. Although some people tip out of genuine gratitude and appreciation, most people tip because it is accepted custom. It is safe to say that tipping is a social habit that we have acquired but have not fully accepted. Tipping is a two-way interchange as well as an exchange. It is an exchange of money for services rendered, but it is also an interchange between people, usually between two people in a face-to-face confrontation. Because it is a personal interchange, it is an emotional one as well, and inherent in it are possibilities for pleasure, satisfaction, irritation, or anger. These emotional possibilities are experienced by both the giver and the recipient; in addition, they represent psychological reactions and produce further psychological reactions.

Tipping is often a means of self-expression for the customer. Such an individual sees it as a measure of personal worth and an indication of material means. He does not necessarily overtip, although he may, but he does tip in a showy or conspicuous manner. A woman rarely tips for self-expression reasons. The man who does is an extrovert, perhaps even a bit of a show-off.

Service people may look on their tips as a measure of their personal worth. Adding up their tips gives them more than a sense of financial accomplishment; it also gives them a sense of having performed a useful service. The quality of service does influence tipping, particularly the size of tips, but not to the extent that many people think it does. The mood of either the customer or the person performing the service can influence the size of the tip, and discrimination of various kinds often enters into the tipping picture, as in the case of one woman who explained: "I always give more to black waitresses because I think they have a harder time in life." Discrimination can also be on the basis of physical appearance, as when a pretty waitress gets a larger tip from a male customer than the homely girl who may actually be a better waitress. A young girl usually has a better chance of getting a large tip than does an older woman. Waitresses usually receive larger tips from men than waiters do. The men may be more efficient and businesslike, but they don't inspire sympathy from those they serve. On the other hand waiters do not have a better chance of getting larger tips from women. A woman who receives good service from a waiter likes to think that his attention to her needs is the result of her charm and personality.

Most women either tip the minimum or less than the minimum. It is not that they are cheap, but psychologically they are more prepared to accept the idea of being served than men are. A woman may wait on her family at home, but when she goes out, she has no trouble in adjusting to being the one who is served. Women, too, are more apt to notice and be critical of service than men. Preparing and serving a dinner is not a mystery to them, for they do it at home all the time. Having it done for them when they eat out is a convenience and a pleasure, but it is not always something for which they feel they should pay extra. Often women will take good service for granted and notice only bad service.

More women than men are concerned about the morality of tipping. They believe that tipping is bad, outdated, and degrading. "When I eat out and pay for a meal," Ann said, "I am also paying for good service. I expect it. The price of a restaurant meal is high enough, I think, to take care of the cost of that service without my having to pay an additional sum. Tipping is just a form of blackmail. Almost, I want to think of my waitress as an employee with some personal dignity, not as a slave that must try to get my favor so I will give her some money. I feel that the employer is responsible. He hired the waitresses. He should pay them an adequate wage and not expect his customers to share in the expenses of his overhead costs!" It is for this very reason that tipping irritates many people. They don't want to go out for a good time and have to face the economic problems of others.

Women are "mood" tippers. If they are feeling happy or satisfied with life, they will leave a good tip, but women who are unhappy, depressed, or not feeling well, will leave small tips or perhaps none at all. They do not undertip out of meanness, but because they are so wrapped up in their own misery or troubles; in some cases they may even be unaware of the service they have received.

The average tipper gives an amount that varies from 10 to 15 percent. He does not tip according to the quality of service; he tips because he has been told that it is good manners to tip. This person is usually well balanced, mature though colorless, and conservative in his views, actions, and opinions. He knows the socially correct thing to do and is a follower rather than a leader. He does not want to be a loner or adventurer but just one of the group. He buys name-brand merchandise, looks at popularly rated television programs, and takes most of his opinions from popular magazine articles.

Undertipping indicates a certain degree of meanness; this is usually both financial and personality meanness. An individual may undertip when he is opposed to tipping on principle but lacks the courage to not tip. An undertipper is often fussy and hard to please. He expects more for his small tip than generous tippers expect and is quick to complain if things aren't to his satisfaction. Undertipping sometimes occurs when the tipper does not feel any necessity to make a favorable impression. This person will give a good tip in a restaurant where he is known but undertip in a strange one to which he does not expect to return. A person's tipping may also be influenced by the company he is in. "I always give a big tip when I'm out with friends because I don't want to look like a cheapskate," one man said. "When I'm alone, I leave a small tip. After all, I don't really care what the waitress thinks of me." The undertipper is more interested in getting than giving. He is self-centered.

There are two kinds of nontippers. One is deliberately stingy and antisocial; the second is intellectually aloof from the usual social customs. The first type of nontipper may not tip because he enjoys putting other people down. He knows that the waitress expects a tip, and he gets pleasure from denying her that expectation. He likes to assert himself as a power or authority figure by saying No to people. He says No to the waitress by not giving her a tip. This same individual, however, expects and demands a lot of service, and his attitude toward his family, friends, and business associates is also very demanding. He continually looks for ways in which he can put them down.

The second type of nontipper is a nonconformist. More self-centered and arrogant than the undertipper, he is usually very self-sufficient and forms his own opinions. He dresses to please his own taste and for comfort and doesn't care what other people say or think about him.

There are also two basic types of overtippers. One is the extreme extrovert who is feeling exuberant and expansive. "Show me a good eater, and I'll show you a good tipper!" one waitress told me. "I especially like to wait on a fat man who has ordered a big meal. He not only has a good time eating but shares that good time with me by leaving a large tip." She also said that festive occasions when people are celebrating some happy event are sources for large tips.

Overtipping can also indicate a lack of self-esteem and feelings of inferiority, particularly social inferiority. A person may have sufficient money to eat in a fancy restaurant or stay in an expensive hotel but not have the background to be at ease while there. He thinks that people are aware of his social ignorance and lapses. He may imagine gestures or facial expressions of contempt from those who serve him. If he sees two people whispering, he imagines that they are discussing his lack of social grace and poise. And although he feels uncomfortable and put down, he will leave an extra-large tip. This may earn him some fleeting gesture of respect; it does enable him to show that he is, at least financially superior.

Overtipping may also come from a desire to be well liked or loved. Lone / people who have doubts about their lovableness, whose personal lives are unsatisfactory in terms of family or love relationships, may try literally to buy the favor and approval of the person who is waiting on them. They may carry this same attitude over into other areas of their lives and try to buy friendship and love with gifts and special acts of attention.

Bellboys in hotels have learned to tell about a guest's personality from the size of tips and the way tipping is done. A guest who comes in with only one suitcase and overtips is likely to try to skip out without paying his bill. So is the guest who takes the lowest-priced room and gives an extra-large tip. A guest who gives an average tip for an average room is an ordinary guest who will obey hotel rules, pay his bill, be quiet and not destructive of hotel property, and not cause the hotel staff any extra work or concern.

To many people, tipping is a form of black-mail extorted to insure adequate service, which should be provided in any case. They tip grudgingly and often out of fear. Tips, to them, are a kind of bribe which they offer to keep harm from themselves or their possessions. This is sometimes considered to be more necessary for some of the service occupations than for others.

"Yes, I always tip my beauty operator," Mrs. S. said. "If I didn't, I'd be afraid to go back and have my hair cut or set."

"I tip the doorman because I'm dependent upon him," explained Mr. C. "I know a man who always refused to tip, and one day the doorman shut the door on his fingers. He said it was an accident, but I just wonder if it really was. I also tip my barber. It's important in my work that I look my best, and I can't take a chance on getting a funny haircut!"

Both Mrs. S. and Mr. C. tipped out of fear.

In today's crowded world, manners are very important, since population density forces us to live in close proximity with others, and manners help us to live peaceably and pleasantly with one another.

You and your manners are inseparable, for manners are the outward revelation of what you are within, and they show the true state of your feelings about others and yourself. Goethe said, "Behavior is a mirror in which everyone shows his image"; manners are a large part of your behavior pattern. Your manners show you as you really are, not as you would like to be or as the person you are pretending to be. Your manners may be telling things about you that you would prefer to keep secret. Looking at your manners is just another way of looking at yourself but with more awareness and perception than your usual quick, superficial glance.

4

Beauty Is Only Cloth-Deep

CLOTHES AND CIVILIZATION

"We could not very well have civilized life without clothes," wrote the eminent English philosopher and mathematician Alfred North Whitehead. There has, in fact, been a determined effort on the part of the so-called civilized nations to put clothes on the less inhibited nations. The best example of this is the ubiquitous mother hubbard, a full loose-fitting gown handed out along with religious tracts by almost every Christian missionary. Putting clothes on the "savages" was considered to be as much of a God-given duty as conversion and baptism.

In addition to their effect on a country's life and society, clothes have a distinct and important psychological effect on the individual. Clothes and personality have a close connection. When fig leaves were the fashion, the only personality characteristics revealed were the then new feelings of modesty and guilt. Since then, however, clothes have become more elaborate and personal emotions more complex. Today personality is revealed in everything you do and in what you own. Your clothes are no exception. They, too, reveal what you are thinking and even occasionally what you are planning. They give clues to your personality, your emotional development, and your degree of maturity.

Why are clothes so important? Why have such apparently simple things as body coverings become moral and social issues? If civilization and clothes are synonymous, as both religionists and philosophers claim, then there must be some potent motivations behind the wearing of clothes. The prime motivation and probably the very first one is the need for some kind of protection against the elements. In this instance we may say that clothes are a part of man's survival kit. Some time back in the most primitive beginnings an inventive early man decided to improve his lot by adding a layer of additional skin. He did this by throwing over his body an animal hide or fur. Or he may have "woven" some kind of garment from leaves or bark. No matter what the material was, the purpose was plain—to increase his comfort and to expand his usefulness. It was a first step toward an assertion of man's authority over nature.

Down through the centuries, then, various items of clothing were developed to help man defend himself against the natural elements. As a result men no longer had to stay in a shelter because of rain, snow, or extreme heat. By wearing the proper protective clothing they were able to extend their working hours and increase the time they spent hunting and foraging for food.

That most famous fictional castaway, Robinson Crusoe, used his ingenuity to make protective clothing and even an umbrella. In modern times we see a variation of this when a sudden rain comes and people improvise protection by placing a newspaper over their head. This improvisation, a sign of adaptability, is one personality trait that you reveal by your attitude toward clothes. Clothes have also been adopted as a form of morality, yet morality in clothing is a variable thing. What has been esteemed as modest to one generation has not interested another generation in its quest for decency. Today there is little concern about morality in dress. Whereas fifty years ago it was not uncommon for ministers to preach on the evils of dress, most of today's religious leaders do not even blink at the miniskirts or hippie styles of their congregants.

In our highly permissive society morality can hardly be considered to be of tremendous importance in deciding what we wear. It would be inconsistent to emphasize modesty and morality in clothing while permitting pornographic movies to be shown and pornographic books and pictures to be sold. A moral code in dress would be in conflict with our permissive standards of sexual behavior.

It is best to remember that in any case morality is not synonymous with honesty. Covering up in public has never been a guarantee of safeguarded public morals. As is known now from various private diaries and other sources, the so-called Proper Victorians while modestly dressed were busily engaged in all kinds of sexual peccadilloes and intrigues. Human nature being what it is, clothing is no guarantee of morality. It can only give an appearance of morality, which is, after all, a completely different thing.

There are other motivations for selecting and

wearing clothes, and these are not so much concerned with the big issues of survival and morality
as they are simply personality preferences and
indicators. It is in these motivations that we see
individualism, self-expression, and sometimes rebellion.

SELF-IMAGE, EMOTIONAL RESPONSES, AND YOUR CLOTHES

Clothes are a means of self-expression. They
are the outward manifestation of your self-image.
They are only one part of your self-image, but they
are an important part because they present to the
world a picture of you, a picture you have prepared by your selection of your clothes. Clothes
are your second skin. They are *you.*

William James wrote in his *Principles of Psychology:*

> In its widest possible sense . . . a man's Self
> is the sum total of all that he can call his, not
> only his body and his psychic powers, but his
> clothes and his house, his wife and children,
> his ancestors, and friends, his reputation and
> works, his lands and horses, and yacht and
> bank account. All these things give him the
> same emotions. If they wax and prosper, he
> feels triumphant; if they dwindle and die
> away, he feels cast down.

Clothes indicate your emotional temperature and
your emotional responses to life. They give a clue
as to how and what you are feeling about things.
They give a psychological profile of your personality.

If you wear loose, comfortable clothes, you are also comfortable with yourself. You relate well to other people. You accept reality and have learned to adjust to life's ups and downs. In general, you are optimistic and adaptable. You are cooperative with others and enjoy good social and family relationships.

Tight, constricting clothing frequently indicates anxiety and tenseness. If you dress this way, you may suffer from feelings of inferiority. You do not mix well in groups. You are often both timid and socially inept.

Carla was not a pretty woman, and she had not compensated by developing charm and an interesting personality. Instead, everything about her suggested plainness, dullness, and tenseness. Anxiety was the only emotion that Carla seemed able to project. It was this anxiety and her deep-seated feeling of inferiority that had brought Carla to my office. Her clothes suggested her personality-adjustment problems. Not only was she dressed in dark, unbecoming colors, but her dress was tight in the sleeves so that she could use gestures in only a limited way. Her constricting clothes forced her to sit in a rigid, unrelaxed position. As Carla's analysis continued, she slowly began to loosen up. This loosening process took place in her posture, her facial expressions, her voice, her gestures, and her clothes. The first change was shown when she wore a blouse that had full sleeves. Later she began to add touches of color and ornamentation to her costume. Throughout her treatment Carla continued to improve both her attitude and her physical appearance. At one point she said laughingly, "I feel rather like a slowly emerging butterfly, Doctor."

Emotional insecurity may also be shown in wearing high-fashion clothes that are not suitable or comfortable. If you choose such clothes, you have low self-esteem. You do not trust your own judgment. You may want to be accepted by the group, but you are not sure enough of what you should do or how you should act. You dress up to hide your feelings of insecurity. Without your high-fashion clothes you feel more than physically naked—you feel emotionally naked.

A number of office supervisors have told me that they frequently have problems with new, inexperienced workers who report for work wearing clothes that would be more appropriate for the dance floor or for dating. "It's usually a matter of ignorance combined with fear that makes girls dress this way," one supervisor said. "Either the offender is quick to notice that none of the other girls dresses that way or one of the older workers explains about proper office dress. In no time at all the new girl has learned that she must get along on the merits of her work and not her wardrobe."

However, women aren't the only ones who have problems related to clothes and personality. Many men are concerned and confused by clothes, particularly the role of clothes and styles in their lives.

"I'm just an ordinary guy!" complained Ed, "so why do I have to dress like a freak?"

Ed had a long list of complaints about men's clothes. Obviously the new fashions weren't for him. On his list were objections to the colors, styles, and what he called the "sissy" look.

Actually in many civilizations men have dressed more colorfully and flamboyantly than women. In some primitive societies men decorate themselves with feathers, tattoos, and special costumes, devices thought to enhance the power of the wearer. It is only in recent times that men have been relegated to the background in clothes, a background from which they are now rather rapidly emerging.

A look at any historical costume book will show men of the past centuries richly and ornately dressed. By the late nineteenth century men's fashions had settled into dreariness, and a kind of universal uniform became the prevailing style. Undoubtedly, the development of men's clothes was meant to parallel the practical and logical development of the entire social and political structure. Also, most men now were seriously engaged in rather prosaic ways of earning their living. The days of the cavalier and the buccaneer were over except for a few adventuresome souls. The dawning of the age of the common man was to mean not only more freedom but also more sobriety and sameness in clothes. This would also be a natural result of the gradual adoption of the idea of the equality of all men.

Equality is now an accepted doctrine, and individualism in men's clothes is returning. It is not always being accepted wholeheartedly and without suspicion, especially among older men. Many have a mistaken idea about the new styles. They are afraid to wear them because they are afraid of their repressed femininity. It is a psychological fact that men and women share qualities of gentleness, and men should not consider this to be a sign of weakness.

A man who has no doubts of his masculinity, has high self-esteem, and feels accepted as a man does not worry about the new styles. He feels

sure enough of himself to wear pastel jackets,
brightly colored shirts, plaid or striped trousers,
and florid ties.

Although both sexes can be sloppy, it is usually
men who resist being well groomed, neatly dressed,
and clean. Just as it is a false assumption that
plain clothes are a sign of masculinity, so is the
idea that dirtiness and sloppiness are equivalent
to masculinity. Some men take pride in looking
unkempt, wearing old clothes, and skipping baths.
To them, smelling strong means *being* strong!

Revenge is often the motive for the man who
refuses to be neat or well dressed. Often this
revenge is directed against his wife. Occasionally
it can be traced back to an anger that is really
directed at his mother. Apparently at some time
during adolescence he resolved to get even with
his mother for her insistence that he wash and
dress up.

"I'm ashamed to go anywhere with my husband," one woman told me. "He simply won't
shave on the weekends or clean up. I tell him
that I don't like living with a pig, but he just
ignores me. I've gotten so I don't invite anyone
to the house, either, because I feel so embarrassed."

Her husband had been educated in a military
school. He had not wanted to leave home and go
away to this school despite its many advantages,
and still resented having been sent to it. He continued to carry his anger against his parents
throughout his adult life. He was actually defying
his mother rather than his wife when he refused
to wash and dress on the weekend.

Carelessness in dress is symptomatic of contempt toward other people, social customs, and

institutions. Individuals who are deliberately unkempt know that people will notice them, and in
many cases they welcome this. It is one way in
which they can express how they feel about life.
What they are saying is, "Go ahead, look at me.
You can see how I feel about you and what you
stand for. I defy your stupid, silly rules of manners and good taste!" These people know that they
are offending others, but they also know that they
can usually get away with it.

This defiance in a woman is shown by wearing
stockings with runs, letting her slip hang out
below her skirt, having a ripped hem, or letting
her brassiere straps dangle. She may also wear
torn or wrinkled clothes and have shoes that are
scuffed and run-down at the heels. Jonathan Swift
in writing about such a woman said, "She wears
her clothes as if they were thrown on her with
a pitchfork."

A man shows his defiance and contempt by
wearing stained and rumpled clothing. He may
refuse to wear a tie or a coat in business or
social situations where such items would be appropriate. His shoes will also have run-down heels
and be unpolished.

The man who goes around with his fly completely or partially unzipped is expressing two things.
He is showing indifference to social customs, and
he is also asking for approval of his masculinity.
He is calling attention to his sexual role. In many
cases this is the only area in which he has shown
any proficiency.

COLOR AND CLOTHES

Color has always had special symbolic meaning in regard to clothes. It also has psychological meaning, since color reflects personality mood.

Traditional ideas about color in clothes may have passed into folklore, but the psychology behind these ideas is still valid. Thus, black was worn for mourning, white signified purity, gold or silver meant wealth, purple was for royalty, and gray was the color favored by older people.

Even today dark colors usually mean depression, and bright colors signify happiness. If you habitually choose dark colors for your clothes, you may be hiding an emotional problem. You feel "heavy" in your mood, and therefore you unconsciously select colors that make you look heavy. Being depressed and anxious, you prefer shadow to sunlight. You want to avoid people. You select clothes that are negative in color and effect. By dressing in drab or dark colors you manage to project your feelings of unhappiness to others.

Bright colors signify lightness, happiness, and joy. If you have a wardrobe that is primarily bright in color tones, you are optimistic, happy, and creative. You have an outgoing personality. You are fond of people and socially minded.

If your dominant colors are beige, dark green, brown, or gray, you are carefully neutral about life. You try to stay away from emotional commitments or involvements of either a personal or a social nature. Although you are kind, you are firm and prefer discipline to disorder. You try to take a logical, nonemotional approach to life, but you sometimes deceive yourself by faulty rationalization.

Blue as the dominant color in your clothes shows that you are easygoing. You have a calm personality and are content with what you have.

Green shows a high degree of awareness and some aggressive tendencies in your personality. You are civic-minded and keep active in various civic and social projects. You show concern for the welfare of others, particularly those less fortunate.

Red indicates activity, leadership, and an expansive personality. Because of your energy, you may also be nervous and overactive. You like sports, games, and good times of all types. You are the life of the party and very popular. People like you because you can make them laugh. You frequently act on impulse, and if things don't turn out the way you expect, you waste little time on regrets but go on to your next project.

If yellow is your dominant clothes color, you are cheerful and lighthearted. You are relaxed and rarely worry. New things and new ideas interest you, and you like to be surrounded by the latest gadgets. Although you are not always persistent in your efforts or interests, you are happy with what you are doing at the moment.

It is possible to use color to get over a particular mood or to convey a desired impression. The next time you feel sad or depressed, look at the color of clothes you are wearing. If you have on a dark or neutral color, change to a brighter color. You may be amazed at what it does for your spirits. Wear bright, "positive" colors on the days you have to make a special presentation. They will help to convey the idea that you have something constructive to offer. Blue or green is a good color to wear when you are attending a committee meeting, for both show an awareness and a co-operative manner.

When we go out socially, we anticipate having a good time, and therefore we dress up in our best clothes. This common custom has led to the slang phrase "glad rags." If you choose the right colors, you can make any of your clothes glad rags.

Wearing colors that clash or are inappropriate for the occasion indicates an emotional problem and in extreme cases may mean mental illness. The color disharmony is an outward symbol of the inward turmoil. The personality fragmentation is expressed by the color fragmentation.

WEATHER AND CLOTHES

If clothes are a part of your survival kit, then your attitude toward weather and clothes can be very informative about your personality and your degree of emotional adjustment to life.

If you are able to adapt to the weather, you show that you have a mature, well-adjusted personality. If you are out and are caught in a sudden storm, your ability to invent some means of weather protection for yourself indicates a high degree of resourcefulness. You are creative and use creativity in all areas of your life.

However, if when a cloud appears in the sky, you go out with raincoat, rain hat, rubbers, and an umbrella, you are overly cautious. You feel insecure as a person. You worry about your health. You anticipate the worst. The fear of death may be a very strong fear in your life. You are probably a hypochondriac, or you may suffer from various psychosomatic illnesses.

I have a neighbor for whom pneumonia is never very far from his life. He has spent years anticipating that he will be struck down by this disease. He will not go out in inclement weather unless it is absolutely necessary. When he does go out, he fortifies himself with cold remedies and bundles up. He has communicated this attitude to his children, and they show signs of continuing this same fearful attitude toward the weather.

By anticipating the worst in weather individuals are exhibiting pessimism. Often they carry over their distrust of the weather to a distrust of people and things in general. They expect to be cheated. Sometimes they have this attitude because of one or more disappointing incidents in the past. They are the people who expect it to rain on weekends or their vacation. They feel sure that their plane trip will be canceled or at least delayed because of bad weather. Good things rarely happen to them because they have trained themselves to think only in terms of disaster and trouble.

A distrust of the weather can also reveal a dislike of yourself and other people. When you find fault with the weather, you may be projecting your dissatisfaction with yourself or others. You are afraid to actually verbalize your true feelings, so you transfer those feelings to a safe neutral force. It can also reveal a lack of self-confidence. You feel helpless and overwhelmed by the problems of daily living. Weather is one of the forces that you feel are not only against you but beyond your control. Weather typifies your inability to manage your life successfully.

Refusing to dress appropriately for the weather may mean an attitude of bravado. It shows a foolish lack of concern about practical matters. Some men think that to go without a hat or coat in rain or other bad weather is a sign of masculinity, a proof of the virility. It is not. It is actually a sign of uneasiness about masculinity. It is not a feminine characteristic to be dressed suitably and sensibly.

Buttons and Bows

Ornamentation in clothes is a direct reflection of man's creativity and ingenuity as well as an expression of his vanity. Aside from enhancing a costume, it can express religious and political views, such as in the wearing of special badges or rosettes. In seventeenth-century England it was possible to tell whether a person was a Roundhead or a Cavalier simply by the degree of ornamentation of his clothes. Some religious groups such as the Quakers, Mennonites, Nazarenes, and the Church of the Brethren have prescribed "plain" dress for their members, with no frivolous ornamentation, which is thought to be too "worldly." Early religious leaders used to warn against the "sin" of too much pride in clothes and excessive ornamentation. Isaac Watts in his *Against Pride in Clothes* wrote, "Let me be dress'd fine as I will, flies, worms, and flowers, exceed me still," and in the same period Lady Mary Wortley Montague suggested, "Be plain in dress, and sober in your diet." Despite these and other admonitions, most people have preferred ornamentation on their clothing. Although the present period is one in which ornamentation is at a minimum, its lack is perhaps compensated for by the use of color and fabrics.

Ornamentation can also be used to express restlessness, a craving for novelty, and a desire for change. We see this today in hippie dress. In the 1940's, which were years of national and world changes and restlessness, there was an upswing toward the fad of ornamentation, which included the use of military motifs and the use of printed photographs on dress fabrics.

If you add to your clothes by tasteful ornamentation, it shows that you have pride in yourself and that your level of self-esteem is high; you are well adjusted and willingly accept your place in life. If you refuse to wear clothes that are decorated with attractive and suitable ornamentation, you are expressing anti-social qualities. You are displaying your hidden fears of other people and social situations. You are showing that you lack self-confidence and have a low level of self-esteem. Your lack of interest in your clothing reflects your lack of interest in things in general. It may also indicate depression and withdrawal tendencies.

Overornamentation indicates emotional insecurity and immaturity. The woman of sixty who wears clothes with ornamentation designed for teen-agers is both foolish and unrealistic. Dressing in young styles will not bring back her youth or necessarily make her more attractive.

Although she was a woman in her forties, Virginia tried to look like a young girl. Her dresses were chosen to emphasize a childlike innocence that she did not possess. She wore lots of bows, ruffles, and frills. Her favorite color was pink. Virginia could not accept herself as an adult. She did not want to have adult responsibilities. It was psychologically significant that she had lived at home with her parents until they died very suddenly as a result of an accident. Soon after that she married an older man who had a protective attitude toward her. She always called her husband "Daddy," although they had no children. He frequently referred to her in endearing terms that would have been more appropriate for a child than for a grown woman. Even in her marriage Virginia was able to keep up the fiction that she was still "Daddy's little girl." Her husband took care of all the details of their financial and business affairs. Virginia played house and instead of dolls, had two pet dogs whom she treated as toys. It is obvious that as she gets older, Virginia will face some rather serious problems of emotional adjustment unless she can learn to take her place in the adult world. Clothes are one area in which she will have to learn to grow up.

IDENTIFICATION AND CLOTHES

There can be both positive and negative identification uses of clothes. In the case of Virginia we have seen a case of negative identification—an unwillingness to dress suitably. It is not unusual to see men and women continue to wear collegiate styles when they have not been in school for at least twenty years. They are trying to recapture through clothes the same feelings of hope, happiness, and anticipation they had then and trying to deny what is for them the unpleasant reality of middle age. Some persons continue to select their clothes to please their parents even after becoming adults themselves. They may do this out of consideration, but more often it is out of fear. Logically they know that their parents can no longer effectively punish them, yet the old childhood fear of parental wrath is still there.

"My mother doesn't approve of the new styles," Elaine said, "and it's not worth having a fuss with her when I buy something she doesn't like. So I pick out things that I know she'll approve of, and it makes life simpler and pleasanter for us all."

There was a certain amount of bitterness mixed in with the tones of resignation, however, as well there might have been, since Elaine was a woman in her late thirties who held a responsible job in a large office. Yet Elaine continued to defer to her mother, not out of respect, but out of fear of unpleasantness.

"I'd like to dress a little more flamboyantly," one man told me, "but my parents would never approve. They are quite conservative, especially my father, and just wouldn't understand."

Women more than men tend to be influenced by the opinion of parents in choosing clothes, and a woman will often identify specifically with her mother in making her own clothes choices. She may select the same styles, colors, or price clothes that her mother does. Part of this can be attributed to the close bond that often exists between a mother and daughter in such areas as clothes, shopping, homemaking, and child care.

If you still select clothes that reflect your parents' interests rather than your own, you have a very dependent personality. Other personality characteristics may be timidity and an inability to come to decisions easily or without help.

On the other hand positive identification in clothes can be very helpful to people who are unsure of themselves and of their taste in clothes. By selecting models who are knowledgeable about clothes they are able to dress in a more becoming and appropriate way. Positive identification is a way in which an individual can learn how to use clothes correctly in order to project a desired image.

Identification is a common process during adolescence when young people seek in every way to emulate their heroes.

Motion-picture stars, television personalities, and socially prominent individuals are all used for clothing identification purposes. Newspapers and magazines report the details of what is worn by prominent people at various social events, and those interested can not only read about the details of the clothes worn but copy them for use in their own wardrobes.

UNIFORMS AND COSTUMES

Many people will purposely choose an occupation or profession in which they can wear a uinform. Uniforms are basically body disguises that also affect personality development and emotional responses. It is not unusual for individuals to respond in one way while in uniform and to respond in another way when out of uniform. A uniform provides a ready-made portable environment for the wearer. It can be a refuge and a barrier behind which he hides. Of course, not all

uniforms have the same psychological appeal
or value. A general's uniform has more status
than the uniform of a doorman, although a quick
glance may show them to be very similar in appearance.

Most uniform-wearers can be divided into two
categories:

In the first group we have those who are low
in self-esteem and have doubts about their own
personalities. They do not have a clear grasp of
their identities and spend much of their time and
emotional strength in searching for themselves.
A typical person in this category depends upon
his uniform for his personality, borrowing his
importance from his clothes. Take away his uniform, and he is lost. A man who needs a uniform
to reinforce his identity will be happy in the
armed forces or police or fire departments. A
woman will choose a career in a field such as nursing. Many times such people do not feel that they,
as individuals, would receive the respect they desire but know that wearing a uniform will insure
them some measure of respect.

In the second group of uniform-wearers we
have those whose low self-esteem is coupled
with timidity and extreme personality dependence. They like the anonymity and protective
coloration of a uniform and receive a needed
sense of security from wearing one.

A man who wore a uniform in his work as a
guard at a local museum told me, "It makes me
feel good. I feel like I belong, and people know
that I am a responsible person, a trusted employee."

Wearing a uniform is an attempt at masquerade, an act of disguising true character. Mas-

querading is a very common and natural human urge. Mentally, we all indulge in some form of masquerading every day, but we usually can't change our appearance. Children regularly play "dress-up," a form of masquerade, and it is an intergral part of their growing-up process. Adults have to confine their masquerading to theater and lodge activities, Halloween parties, fiestas, and fancy-dress balls. All these provide the framework within which we can satisfy our desires to become, if only temporarily, someone we wish we were. Being the Grand Master of a lodge and wearing the elaborate regalia of that office helps many a man to forget for an evening the dullness and disappointment of his real life. Taking part in amateur theatrics helps to compensate for an unexciting personal life. It makes it possible not only to change clothes but to assume for a few hours a totally different personality. Funny costumes allow us to let off steam and express repressed desires. In a costume you don't have to be yourself or be dignified and serious. This is especially true of and explains the popularity of clown costumes.

SEX AND CLOTHES

We have in our culture prevailing and simultaneous attitudes that are in conflict with each other. On one hand we feel the need to cover our bodies; on the other hand we feel the need to display our bodies for sexual purposes. Modesty and shame war with boldness and desire, and since not everyone responds in the same way, we have a variety of clothing styles. These include what we could term both modest and sexually oriented clothing for both sexes.

There has often been ambivalence in our attitude toward clothes. For example, it was presumed that all "good" women dressed modestly and all "bad" women dressed immodestly and provocatively. As many men have found to their surprise, this is not a sure indicator of either sexual interest or sexual ability. Some of our ambivalence about clothes is resolved when we dress modestly at work and in certain social situations but dress much less modestly at home or on the beach.

The styles of today have done much to change some of the old notions about both modesty and sexual morality connected with clothes; the mini-skirt especially has done a great deal toward crumbling the old attitudes. The mini is a symbol not of sexual availability but of the new freedom for women. It is an honest expression of feminine sexuality as well as an expression of equal sexuality with men. Women are not being exhibitionistic when they wear minis; they are merely saying "I like being a woman."

Women who feel unattractive do not like the mini length. Their self-image is one of dowdiness, and they do not mind wearing clothes that make them look dowdy. They may be afraid of sex or regard themselves as sexual failures. If married, their marriage is often unsatisfactory.

Since clothes are a kind of substitute body, they should be used to display your best features and accent your natural sexuality. Individuals who think well of themselves select clothes that will emphasize their good points and hide their bad ones.

An identity crisis in either overt or latent homosexuality will be reflected in clothes. A female homosexual who has strong masculine identification will wear either men's clothes or women's sports clothes which are frankly imitative of male clothing. If, however, she fears her homosexual desires, she will overdress in very feminine styles in an effort to convince herself and others that she is really a woman.

Jan consulted me because she was having a sexual identity problem. In her love affairs she was bisexual; she could not deside whether she wanted to be a woman or act like a man, and this had made her emotionally disturbed. Her behavior was a mixture of both sexes as was her clothing. The first time Jan came to my office she was wearing blue jeans, heavy work shoes, a tailored blouse, and earrings. The general effect even to the uninitiated was one of sexual confusion!

The male homosexual responds in a similar way. If he is afraid of his homosexual impulses, he will stress masculinity in his clothes. He may even dress sloppily to indicate his supposed ruggedness. However, positive identification is shown by the male homosexual who wears styles and colors that do not disguise or deny his true sexual role. Both men and women, heterosexual and homosexual alike, may exhibit sexual willingness in the way they dress. It is usually more common among women, since basically dressing is for most women a gambit in the sexual game. However, male homosexuals will often wear tight form-fitting trousers that emphasize their genitals and buttocks to entice other men.

False virginity is sometimes exhibited by women

and young girls who dress in a style that is meant to suggest innocence and inexperience. This is a deliberate pose which caters to masculine vanity about virginity. As long as men feel that virginity is important, women will resort to trickery to seem to provide that commodity. Sometimes parents are responsible for this pose because they prefer to think of their unmarried daughters as virgins. It works to the mutual advantage of parents and daughters, for parents are less likely to ask question of their daughters if outward appearances conform to their standards of morality.

Transvestism is a sexual deviation in which an individual dresses in the clothes of the opposite sex. It is the ultimate in masquerade. It indicates a confusion of sexual identity and often causes serious problems in social adjustment. The male transvestite wears women's clothing and may also wear a wig and makeup. A female transvestite wears men's clothes, has short hair, and adopts masculine mannerisms. Female transvestites get to satisfy their urges more easily because modern clothing styles for women include so many male-oriented fashions. Many transvestites wear only a few articles of opposite-sex clothing or wear it only at certain times. Frequently a transvestite will wear the underwear of the opposite sex. This is practical, since it is concealed. It is usually ego satisfying and has sexual significance; at times, however, it can lead to social problems. A friend told me that recently she was downtown with another woman, Miss Z. They went to a department store and looked at clothes. Both my friend and Miss Z. found dresses they liked, but Miss Z. refused to try on any clothes. She finally confessed to my friend that she was wearing men's shorts. She said that when she knew she was going to shop for clothes, she always wore women's panties.

As any reader of the daily "advice" columns knows, many men like to lounge around home in lacy lingerie, silk nightgowns, or other articles of feminine attire. Bewildered wives write in, asking what's wrong and what they should do. In most cases they admit that in all other aspects their husbands are satisfactory marriage partners. There is no solution for wives in these cases except to learn to be tolerant and understanding or look for new marriage partners.

A transvestite may be consciously and openly expressing a desire to change his or her sex. Since this is anatomically impossible except by surgery, which is performed only in selected cases, the desired sex role change is indicated by changing clothes. Most transvestites say that they feel more comfortable dressed in opposite-sex clothing. It is a mistaken assumption that all transvestites are homosexual. A study in 1944 by Hirschfeld, published under the title of *Sexual Anomalies and Perversions*, stated that a survey showed that only 35 percent of the transvestites studied were homosexual. Fifteen percent were bisexual, another 15 percent were basically asexual, and the remaining 35 percent were heterosexual. In heterosexuals transvestism is usually a form of fetishism in which the clothing of the opposite sex is used to arouse sexual feelings.

"I am sexually impotent," a male patient confided to me, "unless I put on some article of feminine clothing. This always arouses me sexually, and I am able to have intercourse without any difficulty." He would wear a brassiere or a pair of silk panties or even occasionally a lace-trimmed slip or frilly blouse.

The desire to cross-dress usually shows up in children. Although it is natural for both boys and girls to experiment briefly with clothing of the opposite sex, prolonged attachment to opposite-sex clothing indicates emotional problems and gender confusion. Parents should be aware of the difference between normal childish curiosity, dressing-up play, and emotional involvement with sexual deviation patterns. Most adult transvestites have a history of childhood cross-dressing. Children who suffer from disorders of gender identity can be helped by professional guidance.

One obvious solution to both the problems and the mystique of sexually oriented clothes is the adoption of the "new" look in clothes, the phenomenon of unisex. Unisex, also known as intersex, is the depolarization of the male and female roles; it is sexual homogenization with a blurring of the traditional sex roles and feelings. This criss-crossing of sex roles has meant a crisscrossing of fashions as well, for men and women in the unisex culture dress alike. They do not wear distinctive sexual ornamentation or seek to attract sexual partners through dress. Unisex has proved to be particularly popular in the United States where it has become a favorite tool of many women's liberation groups. They have welcomed unisex as a way of demonstrating the absolute equality of the sexes. Sexual activity has not diminished with the wearing of unisex clothes, for "sameness" has come to mean a closeness that "opposites" used to mean, at least for today's under-thirty group. It may well be that unisex, while deemphasizing the artificial sexual indicators like clothes, has put the emphasis back on the basic and natural sexual differences. The result could be fuller and more total feelings of sexuality.

WOMEN'S LIBERATION AND CLOTHES

Women's clothes have frequently been used throughout history to keep women in their "place." Such clothes often emphasized the sexual role of women and their supposed weakness and helplessness. A fashion with a distinctly anti-feminine slant, for instance, was the hobble skirt, fashionable between 1910 and 1924, which prevented women from walking fast or naturally. It was a long skirt which narrowed at the ankles and psychologically, at least, was very similar to the Chinese custom of binding women's feet. It symbolically kept women from running away.

Who, after all, decrees the new fashions and the changes in clothing styles? Who designs clothes that would indicate and promote the idea of the subservient role of women? The new fashions are decided and promoted by a small group of designers, mostly men, and they exert an influence totally out of proportion to their numbers. Many of these male designers actually have a dislike for women. This dislike may stem from envy, a childhood trauma, feelings of sexual inferiority, or combination of these emotional and psychological factors. Many of the designers exhibit latent homosexual tendencies, and some of them are openly homosexual.

"I used to play with my sister's dolls and make clothes for them," one designer told me. "I always envied my sister and the way she could dress. Because of my interest in women's clothes, I decided to go into fashion design, and now instead of dolls, I have live women to dress." He admitted that he got a vicarious satisfaction out of seeing women wear the clothes he had designed.

Another designer admitted that he secretly envied women their femininity. He resented women because they could have children and felt that this ability to become pregnant conveyed upon them a special creativity. Because he felt this envy and hostility, many of his fashion creations were actually unflattering to women. This was his revenge.

Many of these designers enjoy putting women down because of their feelings of hostility toward their own mothers. What they are saying is, "Look, Mother, I had to do what you said when I was little, but now I'm the boss, and you and other women are going to do what I tell you to do!"

Rebellion has occurred among women from time to time, and the clothing reforms that they instigated have gradually been adopted by other women and by the designers. These periods of rebellion have coincided with demands for women's rights and an end to male domination. In 1851 Amelia Jenks Bloomer insisted that women's clothes and women's rights were related. Mrs. Bloomer, a pioneer in various reform movements including that of women's liberation, is most often remembered for her adoption of the bloomer costume, a short skirt and loose trousers gathered and buttoned at the ankle, often worn with a coat and wide hat. This costume was considered to be more appropriate wear for the "new" woman who was making insistent demands for the vote and other measures of equality.

By 1900 ready-to-wear clothes had become an important feature of the American clothing scene for women and resulted in another example of emancipation in fashion. This was the introduction by American tailors of the shirtwaist, which was a blouse to be worn with a skirt. The shirtwaist, first introduced in 1890, became so popular with American women that by 1910 the production of shirtwaists by commercial firms was a business that employed thousands and took in profits that were in the millions. Although this style of shirtwaist and skirt was attacked by the fashion designers of Europe, particularly those in Paris, American women continued to demand and wear shirtwaists and skirts.

Not only was this new style more sensible and comfortable, but to many women it seemed to typify the role that they were beginning to assume and that they coveted. One very practical reason for its popularity was the ease with which it could be cared for in a world that did not have present-day laundry and cleaning facilities. The early twentieth-century woman was starting out to make her way in the business and factory world; she needed practical and easy-to-care-for clothes. Furthermore, the shirtwaist was thought by many to be less feminine and therefore less provocative and more suitable for women who had to work alongside men.

Today's woman also has her say about fashion. The controversy over the midi length was a good example. Women showed a healthy resentment against this foolish and dictatorial fashion change, thus indicating a high level of consciousness of their own self-image. There were several sides to this confrontation between women and the designers. One was economic. Perhaps at a time when women did not buy their own clothes they were not averse to getting a new wardrobe whenever the fashions changed. Now, however, few women have fathers or husbands who buy all their clothes. Most women assume all or partial responsibility for the cost of their clothes, and they resent being told to literally throw their money away by tossing out clothes that are still usable.

"My mini-style clothes are still good and attractive," complained one woman. "Why should I get rid of them just because some man says throw everything out of your closet? Besides, I'd rather keep my old clothes and get a new color television!"

Another side to this controversy is the psychological one. Arbitrary fashion changes cause injury to the femal personality. Women do not like to feel that they are being manipulated and controlled. They resent being told that their judgment is faulty or wrong. They resent being made to feel that it is necessary for them to respond in a childlike way to men's whims about styles.

Women's liberation is just one part of the fashion picture, which, combined with the hippie subculture, increased technological advances in fabrics, and the continuing breakdown of our traditional socioeconomic standards, can mean only continuing revolutions in fashions for both women and men.

YOUNG PEOPLE AND FASHION TODAY

The clothing of today's young people is an expression of rebellion against an ugly world, a sign of group togetherness, and an expression of beliefs. Clothing as an expression of philosophical ideas is not new. Following the French Revolution, it was considered good taste to dress in a simulated peasant costume, thus showing sympathy with the revolutionary ideas of equality. When socialism first became a popular idea, young intellectuals adopted the clothing of working-class people to demonstrate sympathy with the laboring class and to turn away from the middle and upper classes. Jeans, for example, were cheap working trousers until they were taken over and adopted by a large segment of the population. However, while the pseudopoor may enjoy wearing such clothes, the genuinely poor usually yearn to be able to discard their clothes and wear the clothes of the more affluent.

An interesting recent development in fashion has been that many of the styles of the young rebels have been picked up by designers and passed along as fashion ideas to members of the establishment. Most young people today are ignoring the styles suggested by designers and working out their own styles which fit in with their philosophy and orientation. "It's an organic style," one young girl explained to me. "It's an evolving, living expression of what we feel and think." Also, boys as well as girls are deciding on their own styles; no longer are girls the only ones to set a youth trend.

Whether or not parents can agree with their offspring that clothes are a form of communication, they can agree that the new styles reflect the uneasiness between the generations. Today the popularity of the hippie style represents a widespread protest against the establishment. Parents find that they are being overlooked and overruled as their offspring dress up and drop out of conventional society. Those adolescents who do not want to or cannot leave home leave their parents symbolically by adopting hippie clothes.

"I don't recognize my children anymore!" is an increasing cry heard from bewildered parents. Probably at no other time in our history have there been such wide differences between adults and young people, and because of these differences, young people feel compelled to adopt clothes that symbolize their disenchantment with modern civilization. They are also trying to express disillusionment and disgust with the emphasis on materialism that they feel has caused the problems of the world.

PARENTS, CHILDREN, AND CLOTHES

Before the nineteenth century children were dressed in miniature versions of adult fashions. Since then, children have had their own styles, a situation that coincided with the view of children as individuals with special problems and interests and not just small adults.

The area of children's clothing is one that has important psychological overtones. It is an area of adult domination that can end up as a weapon in a psychological and emotional war between parents and children. Children and adolescents may express hostility by deliberately soiling or tearing clothes or by a refusal to hang up or otherwise care for them. Teen-agers often use sloppiness as a weapon against their parents. It is one of the few ways in which they can express rebellion against adult authority.

Even a very young child can quickly become aware of the importance that his parents, particularly his mother, attach to his clothes and the way he is dressed. Therefore, when he is angry with his mother, he can punish her by destroying the things—that is, the clothes—that she seems to put so much emphasis upon. "Getting dirty" is a revenge action in some cases, but in other cases it may be an attention-getting device. The child who feels unloved by his mother knows that he can get a response from her if he dirties his clothes.

On the other side of the battle, children's clothing can express adult domination when mothers insist on dressing their children to please themselves. Such mothers also reveal something about their own personalities. They show how they feel about themselves and how they feel about their own childhood experiences, and they reveal repressed hostility or sexual feeling.

"I never got to wear pretty clothes when I was a child," one mother told me, "so now I really enjoy dressing my little girl."

In this case the little girl didn't always want to dress in "pretty" clothes for her mother, who kept her from playing by saying, "You don't want to get those lovely clothes dirty, do you?"

"You'll dress the way I say, or you'll stay home," one mother told her teen-ager. Naturally, angry words followed this scene, for the mother was determined to have her way, and the youngster wanted to dress as her peers did. Although children need guidance in selecting clothes, they should be permitted some degree of self-expression and autonomy.

A mother who resents being a women will often dress her girl child in boyish clothes. Or she may concentrate on dressing the boys in the family and be indifferent to how her girls dress. A woman who has sexual problems and does not feel either sexually satisfied or sexually adequate will dress her girl children in mature styles. She will push them toward adulthood and sexual fulfillment by dressing them in unsuitable, provocative ways. She will want her daughter to wear a brassiere long before the child needs one. She will also want her to wear adult accessories and make-up at an early age. Because she is dissatisfied with her own adult life, she deprives her child of a normal childhood by refusing to let her dress according to her age level.

Look-alike outfits for mother and daughter are emotionally unhealthy and psychologically unsound. The mother who dresses her child this way is using the child to enhance her own personality and is showing excessive domination and possessiveness. She is robbing the child of her individuality by insisting that she become a replica of herself. There is also a certain coyness in the fact that the mother may be subconsciously proclaiming, "Yes, I'm a mother, but I'm just a child at heart. I'm really younger than you think I am!" She is resisting motherhood and trying to make a baby sister out of her own child.

"There must be some mistake; I wanted a boy" (or a girl), some mothers and fathers exclaim when they are told the sex of their new baby. Most parents, even when disappointed, usually become quickly reconciled and are willing to change their preconceived ideas and plans. A few, however, do not accept the reality of the situation. Mrs. G. was such a mother. She had decided early in her pregnancy that she wanted a girl. Despite her doctor's warnings, she planned exclusively for a female child. When her baby was a boy, Mrs. G. refused to acknowledge that fact. She insisted on referring to the baby in feminine terms. To carry out her wishes, she dressed him in girls' clothes. When he became old enough to go to school, she was forced to come to terms with reality; she continued, however, to dress him in clothes that were feminine in style. She also permitted him to dress up in her old clothes.

A father who wanted a boy but had a girl insisted that she be treated as a boy. He bought her such things as cowboy outfits and a play soldier suit.

Since we are to some extent conditioned by what we wear, it is easy to see that gender confusion was created in these situations.

"I didn't know I was a girl until I was about thirteen," a patient told me. "My parents treated me just like my two brothers. I dressed in their old clothes. I played the same games. I thought I was just a different kind of boy, since I didn't have a penis. When I first began to menstruate and realized what being a girl meant in terms of pregnancy and motherhood, it was a terrible emotional shock. I felt so confused about my sexual identity. I felt like a boy, I usually dressed as a boy, but I had undeniable physical proof that I was a girl."

It took several years before my patient was able to really establish the correct self-image, and this was only accomplished after she sought professional help.

Until recently, it was easily possible to meet a man or a woman and from their clothes deduce their occupations, economic level, and social status. The world was divided into blue-collar and white-collar workers. The rich looked rich and the poor looked poor. Everybody had a place and knew it, and everybody had a role and dressed for it. Now, although it is not so simple to tell occupation and status, it is easier to look for personality traits. People are no longer hiding behind a facade of costume; they are expressing themselves more directly.

You express yourself every day when you get dressed. You show other people something about yourself and your emotions. You reveal a glimpse of your true self and express hidden wishes.

You and your clothes are an important part of your ability to be happy. If you have a sensible attitude toward clothes, it means that you have a sensible attitude toward life, and being at ease with your choice of clothes means that you are also at ease with your own personality. Not only can your mirror tell you how you look in your clothes, it can also tell you what your mood is and how you really feel about yourself.

5

Dream Castles and the
Mortgage of Reality

SHELTER AND INSTINCT

It is commonly supposed that primitive men first took refuge in natural caves. Caves proved to be particularly important for safety; with one entrance which could be blocked the cave was the answer to the danger of nighttime attack. But caves are limited and localized, and later on men began to build shelters that embodied the best features of the cave, shelters that were hidden, perhaps almost inaccessible to those who did not know about them, warm, and with one controllable entrance. Simple structures made of brush and skins evolved into tents and later more permanent and durable buildings.

The home of the city dweller of the future may again be the one that embodies the best features and safety elements of the cave. Feeling safe within the home is a prime necessity, and if violence continues as a part of big-city living, it may dictate the kind of dwellings people in those areas choose for living quarters. Even now, it is considered important to have controlled entrances and exits for a city dwelling so that the inhabitants cannot be taken by surprise, attack, robbed, or murdered. In some new high-income apartment buildings today a visitor is not even permitted in the elevator until the desk clerk has telephoned the tenant whom the visitor claims to be seeing.

But housing is more than shelter and protection; it is an emotional place. "Home" is a psychological experience as well as a physical place.

Not everyone agrees on what a house or a home should be. Some describe it matter-of-factly; some in sentimental terms. Le Corbusier stated that "a house is a machine for living in" while Oliver Wendel Holmes wrote:

> Where we love is home,
> Home that our feet may leave,
> but not our hearts.

But whatever the many opinions about house and home, there is one undeniable fact: Houses reflect the personalities of their owners and occupants. In addition, personality traits are revealed by styles of living and attitudes toward housing.

SELF-IMAGE AND HOUSING

Your house or apartment is more than just the place where you live; it is also an indicator of your self-image, that internal picture you have of yourself, which may not be the same as the actual self you show to others or match the picture others have of you. Your self-image may be an idealized version of your personality, or it may be a faulty image which reflects your lack of self-esteem and self-confidence.

Because our living areas are so tied up with our emotional responses, we tend to seek out houses or apartments that correspond with our personal emotional barometer, our self-image indicator. The person who sees himself as a quiet, conservative, solid citizen usually tries to live in a house that reflects that same quiet conservatism. He is not interested in the flamboyant, the spectacular, or the split-level; he wants to convey the impression of stolidity. On the other hand the person whose house is modern and up-to-date is usually modern and progressive in his views.

People who live in the new suburbs are people with few self-image problems. They have usually chosen this type of housing because they feel at ease in this kind of surrounding. By and large, suburban dwellers are happy in their carefully cultivated developments, and their neat homes and gardens reflect their own self-images as bright, earnest, hardworking citizens.

What does living in one of these chosen neighborhoods show about your personality? For one thing you are socially oriented and like people; happiness for you is the neighborhood barbecue, the shared playground, the community swimming pool, and the cocktail parties and dances at the nearby clubhouse. You also like convenience, and you don't want to have to put up with the vagaries of the plumbing, wiring, or construction of the older home. Just as, at a quick glance, you may bear a distinct resemblance to your neighbor, so your house will only be distinguished from his by some minor details, for you are less interested in individualism and character and more interested in presenting the image of group conformity. You like being surrounded by people of similar tastes, ideas, and living standards; you feel happier and safer. Although modern and progressive to a degree, you are not extreme in any of your opinions because you value group approval more than independent thought. With pride in your home and surroundings you live in happy isolation from the world outside your suburb.

Self-image problems show up when you overbuy or underbuy in housing. People who have strong feelings of insecurity which are emotional in origin may try to bolster their sagging self-esteem and poor self-image by buying a large house or renting an expensive apartment. They are trying to use some exterior force to convey a hoped-for image. "I thought if I had a swanky address," Lance said, "people would respect me more. I figured that they would think I had what it takes to get ahead in the world." He went on to say that he still, despite his new address lacked self-confidence and felt nervous in social situations.

"I really can't afford to live here," Ray said, gesturing toward the high-rise apartment building where he lived, "but I wanted to impress the people I work with." Ray did not feel completely adequate in his job and tried to cover up by living beyond his means. He also drove an expensive car and was heavily in debt. His self-image was not in keeping with the realities of his life.

Individuals with low self-esteem may also express that poor self-image by underbuying in housing; even when they can afford it, they are willing to settle for less because they feel worthless and insignificant. They deliberately live in cramped, unsatisfactory homes. They have a strong desire to treat themselves badly, to be uncomfortable. Unconsciously, they may be punishing themselves for some real or imaginary misdeed. Any person who is living in a house or apartment that is much too small for his needs when he could afford a larger one should take a second look at his self-image and check the level of his self-esteem. If you don't really like yourself, you won't see any necessity to live pleasantly or even comfortably.

Ellen, a patient being treated for depression, lived in a rundown basement apartment which was damp, poorly furnished, and lacking in conveniences. Her reasons for choosing this particular apartment were revealed during the course of her analysis. A disastrous marriage had recently ended in divorce, and Ellen felt shamed by her inability to make a success of her marriage. She blamed herself, and she felt that others, particularly her relatives, blamed her also. Taking this small, dreary apartment was a form of self-punishment, for she had decided that she shouldn't live in as nice a place as she had when she had been married. When, through treatment, Ellen got the proper perspective on her divorce and her life, she was able to move to a more suitable apartment because she had lost her desire for punishment and regained her self-esteem.

MOTIVATION, PERSONALITY, AND HOUSING

Your motivation in selecting a house may be obvious or it may be hidden, unclear even to yourself. Any choice may be conscious or unconscious, and the sum total of your various motivations for your choices and actions makes up the dynamics of your behavior. In most cases the reasons behind the kind of housing you choose go beyond the basic or primary motivation of seeking shelter. A man who is achieving personal and financial success will be motivated to seek better living quarters for his family. His motivations will be compounded of pride, exhibitionism, and some desire for self-indulgence.

A desire to impress others, a wish for self-punishment, and an attempt to cover up for personal inadequacies are some of the obvious motivations for selecting a certain kind of housing. Some that are not quite so obvious are as revealing about personality traits.

There is the person who remains in the old family home; it may have been his grandparents' home, and it was his parents' home. It is old and usually not very convenient. The neighborhood in which it is located is old and established, although often it is slowly becoming increasingly less desirable. Usually that fact as well as the inconveniences of the house itself are ignored by the owner, who refuses to sell and move away. He is probably conservative in his views and opinions and would like to either retain the status quo or go back to the past—nostalgia for the "good old days" is one of his chief characteristics. He resents and may even try to resist change. Family-oriented and family-centered, he takes pride in the accomplishments of family members, even distant relatives, and this pride goes back to encompass the past. Living in the old family home may also indicate a certain degree of timidity and a desire to withdraw from reality. It may also indicate an unwillingness to leave home, an emotional inability to leave the parents even after they have died. When the old family home is one that has belonged to the wife, it usually indicates a strong emotional dependence upon the parents, particularly the father. "I was always Daddy's little girl," Mrs. T. said. "I kept house for him when Mother died, so naturally when I married, we just lived there with him. After he died, it didn't seem right to move away. I felt that I was closer to him if we stayed there." Mrs. T. admitted that she was having some marriage problems over this because her husband wanted to move to one of the suburbs where they could have a more suitable social life.

A man who lives in the old family home may have a fear of the outside and a strong dependence on his family reputation. He may follow the same business or occupation his father did before him. As an individual he feels inadequate and frequently impresses other people as having a negative personality. He is an adult who has grown up physically but not emotionally.

Some people, however, deliberately choose an older family-type home that has no emotional or prior connection with their lives. This action reveals some interesting things about their motivations and their personalities. To them an old house represents security and stability in an emotional sense. It is a tie with the past, the past of a society and culture that they feel they need for strength in their lives.

This is what Alice and John did when they purchased an old, rambling three-story house near the center of town. Their choice puzzled many of their friends, for Alice and John were a young couple in their early thirties with two small children. John was a successful engineer who had a good position with a future. He explained why they had chosen the house. "It was a reasonable price, close to my office, and it has an air of permanence about it. I think this is important in today's world. I can give my children all the things they need, but I also want to give them a sense of the past. I hope that living in this house will give them a kind of stability that is too often lacking in modern life. I wish it really were my old family home, but we moved around so much when I was a kid that I can't even remember some of the places."

Old houses for Alice and John represent oases of security and emotional satisfaction in the modern world. At the opposite end of the scale are those people who absolutely refuse to own a home; they are chronic renters and may also move frequently. Such a person may have a very outgoing personality with a happy, contented disposition. Usually he is more interested in enjoying life than in coping with responsibilities, particularly the responsibilities of home ownership. He doesn't want to be bothered with details or decisions. Some chronic renters have doubts about their ability to cope with emergencies and areas of responsibility. Many of these people prefer to live in large apartments because they feel happier and more secure when they are surrounded by other people. They are basically "hive" people.

Large apartment complexes give a sense of emotional as well as physical security to tenants because these complexes have many of the features of small towns. With their living units, shops, restaurants, and other commercial establishments they furnish the same-size population, diversion of people, and opportunities for leisure and closeness to work as the average small town did. "I could go for weeks without actually leaving my apartment building," one man told me. "There's a drugstore, grocery, two restaurants, a movie theater, bowling alley, laundry, shoe-repair shop, three dentists, and several doctors."

Future plans for large apartment buildings are to include all the necessities of life within a single building or group of buildings, including offices. It is thus conceivable that a person could live his entire adult life in the confines of an artificial atmosphere, working, living, and playing in a circumscribed physical area. This is going beyond the sheltered workshop idea to the completely sheltered life. Psychologically, the difficulty with this scheme is that these persons will gradually lose their ability to adapt to different or changing conditions. In time they will truly become the prisoners of their environment because they are unable to cope with changes, especially change of an abrupt or emergency nature.

For most apartment dwellers, however, it is more often a choice based on a desire to live well and conveniently without the problems and responsibility of physical upkeep. By reducing their shelter problems to a minimum they free themselves for other, more interesting activities and spare themselves much tension and anxiety. I have heard apartment dwellers say, "I don't have to spend any of my time taking care of things. When something goes wrong, I just pick up the telephone and call the superintendent." Living in an apartment can give you great emotional satisfaction if you are the type of person who likes to have others work for you. It can give you the illusion of having numerous servants and vast resources at your command.

Mobile-home living is a compromise between the conventional home and the apartment, an attempt to compromise between the fixed abode and the temporary dwelling. The mobile-home owner has an ambiguous attitude toward responsibility and is perhaps undecided about owning a regular house. A mobile home, he feels, gives him the best of both worlds, for he has a home and a small yard and also the option and possibility of taking his home and moving away when he wants to. For people who have jobs that require frequent moves the mobile home is one of the best solutions for them because it enables them to maintain a semblance of home continuity, even though they must move at repeated intervals. For small children, living in a mobile home may provide emotional security, even though the home itself is moved to a different geographic location.

If you are a mobile-home owner, you probably are an extrovert, friendly and gregarious; no walls or fences shut you away from your neighbors. Not only are you happy with the compactness and orderly arrangement of your mobile home, you also like the community spirit and life in the mobile-home park.

ANTICONVENTIONAL HOUSING

Young adults may show their feelings of rebellion and dissatisfaction by choosing and living in housing that is an affront to their parents. What they are saying to their parents is, "Look, I can do what I want now, and I am not going to live the way you do. I'm turning my back on the things that you consider important and valuable."

Many parents today are baffled and repulsed by the indifference that young people show for what was formerly considered to be "proper and suitable" housing. As one mother put it, "I just don't understand. My children were raised in decent, clean surroundings with every advantage and every convenience, and now they have left home and they live like animals! My son is in a rural commune, no running water, no electricity, and no orderliness; my daughter lives in a dirty walk-up apartment, walls covered with wild posters, no decent furniture, and it is in such a poor neighborhood that I expect the worst each time I go to see her. Why do they insist on living that way?"

It was difficult to discuss the subject with her, for like many other troubled parents, she did not want to face the fact that her children had turned their backs on home, parents, and the whole general social culture. Because home has such an emotional and psychological significance, these young people feel it is important to start one aspect of their protest against society by attacking the home itself. The best way to do that is to live in way that is antipathetic to the members of the regular society whom they are scorning.

In the hippie culture housing as well as furnishings have been reduced to a bare minimum, for here only protest counts, not convenience or cleanliness. Although the emphasis on community life and group cooperation is commendable in many ways, the overall effect is more often than not nullified by the dirt and disease. It is significant that when hippies speak of their living quarters they call them crash pads, words that are expressive but not in any way tender or loving.

Not all forms of rebellion are carried to such extremes, and sometimes the rebellion is mild, yet the emotional feelings are intense. This is the way Joan and Jeffrey felt, and as Jeffrey explained it, their choice in housing was a form of rebellion. "I can't stand those suburban paradises," he said, "and neither can Joan. True, we both grew up in that kind of an environment with everybody doing the same thing at the same time. All of the houses were like so many neat little packages, set in neat little yards with so many feet of flowers, so many square yards of grass, a picnic table, outdoor barbecue, and a jungle gym for the kids. My little girl's dollhouse has more imagination than that! Anyway, we decided that our children should have a chance to express themselves!"

Jeffrey and Joan asserted their individuality by designing and building their own home. It was not only modern but stark in comparison with the homes of their parents and their contemporaries. Their home was a form of protest against the past—a protest against what they considered to be the mindless group conformity of the average person.

If you live in a house like the one that Jeffrey and Joan built, you are proclaiming to the world that you are not like everybody else, that you are an intellectual, a liberal, artistic. You may scorn public opinion but only up to a safe point. Although you may reject the past and tradition, you are interested in making and creating traditions of your own, customs that you feel are suited to your own times and situation. You have both a social conscience and an impatience with non-creative persons or low achievers. You respect and court the approval of those whom you consider to be your intellectual equals.

Dreams versus Realities

The phrase "dream house" is very much a part of our semantic culture. It has emotional and psychological connotations. The very word "dream" implies fantasy and unreality. House, on the other hand, is a concrete, tangible object. Implicit between the two is some amount of conflict. Realtors and advertisers continually offer dream houses for sale, but of course a "dream house" is a highly individual concept. There is always, for most people, a gap between the dream house and the actual house. Most people can live with this discrepancy; a few, however, always remain discontented and may spend their lives working and searching for the ideal house.

Many of our unrealistic ideas about our homes come from our childhood and adolescence; this is particularly true for girls who "play house" and are interested in homemaking, but boys, too, will often plan future homes. It's a long way, though from dream castles to the mortgages of reality, and unless you can learn to accept what is feasible in your living arrangements, you are going to be unhappy. If you are discontented because you cannot have a mansion, that all you can afford is a six-room house, you are behaving in an immature, unrealistic way; you are behaving like a child.

Mavis almost ruined her marriage with her

excessive nagging about a larger house. "But we don't need more room," her husband said in bewilderment. "I can't afford a larger mortgage, and besides there's just the two of us. I don't understand what she wants!"

What Mavis wanted in her own words, was "a real big house surrounded by an iron fence and with a formal garden"—a fantastic wish in terms of the reality of her life. Her husband was a good provider, but his earning power was limited by his lack of training for a more professional position. Where had Mavis gotten her idea, her "dream house"? It turned out that her idea was based on a house in her hometown which she used to pass on the bus. She admitted that as a little girl she had decided that when she grew up, she would have a house just like that one. Mavis did grow up in one sense but not in another, and she refused to face truth in her life.

The mansion–iron-fence complex is not unusual, and unless it is resolved, it can cause unhappiness and misery. If you are a victim of your childhood dreams, stop fantasying and postponing your life; put away your dream castle as you have put away your other toys. Dream houses are fine as dreams and ideals, but you have to be able to accept the reality of your life. If you have a mature personality, then you will have adjusted successfully to any differences between your dream house and your actual living conditions.

Many concepts about dream houses come from parents, and even as adults some people find they are trying to please them when they select a house. "I wanted a split-level home," one man told me, "but my parents were so opposed to it that I changed my ideas. They said it was much

more sensible to have everything on one floor."
Your parents may also pass on certain standards
that cause guilt feelings if they are not lived up
to. A young woman who moved to the city and
lived in an apartment chose one that had a small
balcony where she could have some flower boxes
and plants. "My family always believed that you
had to have some land and a garden," she explained. "This was the best I could do, and I
really am paying more rent than I should, but I
want them to approve of my city life."

Some people, on the other hand, feel guilty if
they achieve their dream house and surpass their
parents in terms of housing. They feel that having a big house while their parents continue to
live in one that is smaller and less adequate is
disrespectful.

HOME GADGETS

This is a gadget-oriented country, and to many
people gadgets are synonymous with American
progress and know-how. Gadgets can be useful,
ingenious, attractive, and handy as well as time-
savers. Gadgets aren't wrong, but the owners of
gadgets are wrong when they let gadgets assume
an emotional importance far out of proportion to
their proper place, as many people do.

Gadgets should be simply conveniences or in
some cases fun objects, but they should not be
love objects. Unfortunately, however, household
gadgets and home furnishings often become substitutes for human love. They may be offered to
others in place of love and intimate personal concern; sometimes they are accepted and even

preferred to more personal expressions of love.

"My husband is very generous and gives me everything I could possibly need," said one wife, "but he never really pays much attention to me. He's always bringing home some new gadget or cooking appliance, but he doesn't really seem to enjoy being at home with me. Sometimes I feel that all these gadgets are just bribes to keep me contented and quiet!" It is unfortunately true that some husbands will give their wives every material object but not themselves. In some cases they are unable to sustain a loving relationship with another person and use gifts to hide this personality deficiency and to forestall any criticism that they are not kind or loving to other people.

Gadgets are sometimes used in marriage to avoid areas of confrontation. This is particularly true when a marriage partner buys gadgets he claims to use for a hobby and becomes so busy with them that it precludes any attempts at communication. Mr. Smith has a complete workshop in his basement, and he uses all his tools and woodworking equipment designing and making things. When he is not busy doing that, he is cleaning and arranging his tools or studying a catalog to see what else he can buy. Upstairs, Mrs. Smith sits forlornly and wishes for some stimulating companionship. She is not amused when well-meaning relatives say, "At least you know where he is and what he is doing!" Yes, she does know that, but she doesn't really know him. Mr. Smith is using his workshop as a means of avoiding a meaningful relationship with his wife.

In a similar case in which I treated the wife for symptoms of depression and anxiety the husband also had to be treated before the wife could be helped and the marriage saved. He had turned to woodworking almost to the exclusion of other activities. To his wife he said little, and he seemed to avoid her. During treatment he finally admitted that he was trying to avoid his wife because he had fears regarding his sexual adequacy. After one or two unsatisfactory sexual experiences he had turned to woodworking as a substitute. He said that working with tools made him feel masculine and strong and that he knew he could succeed in doing with them what he wanted to do. He had not discussed his feelings or fears with his wife, nor had he stopped to consider how she might interpret his neglect of her.

The spouse who insists on buying some expensive but unneeded gadget is punishing his partner. Phil "punishes" his wife by spending all the extra family money on gadgets for his stereo system. When Mary quarrels with her husband or becomes irritated with him, she buys some useless gadgets that he will have to pay for when the monthly bills come in. This makes her feel better at the time she buys them, but since the bills themselves often provoke a quarrel, it has become an endless chain of unhappiness. Mary and Phil are displaying childish immaturity in their attitude toward and use of gadgets. They use gadgets not as material objects but as emotional symbols in a constant psychological war.

Surrounding yourself with gadgets indicates emotional insecurity and is often a cover-up for feelings of loneliness. The less satisfaction you have in your personal life, the more things you need to satisfy your longing for affection. You feel that your gadgets, although inanimate, at least respond to your wishes. This may be closely allied to a desire to control people and situations; when you cannot do this with any degree of success with other people, gadgets can provide you with an opportunity for control and manipulation. Mr. F., who was disappointed in his work situation where he had not been able to advance to the supervisory position he wanted, had a house filled with gadgets. He particularly liked those of an electronic nature, the kind where he could push a button or snap a switch and have something done for him. He liked to talk about his electric garage-door opener, his remote television control, and the timers that turned his lights off and on. Mr. F. enjoyed the illusion of power that those gadgets gave him, for he felt he was a failure in other areas of his life.

People who attempt to bolster their self-image with gadgets are usually not realistic; life has become a form of playacting to them, and the gadgets are part of the stage setting—they are props. Frequently gadgets acquired merely to reinforce the ego are not actually used for any practical purpose; they are pushed aside and forgotten, left to collect dust or to be finally given away to a rummage sale.

The kind of gadgets that you buy also reveals interesting facts about your personality and your problems. The man who feels the necessity of impressing others but is deficient in self-esteem will buy gadgets he thinks are status symbols. These have to be gadgets that can be easily seen or readily demonstrated—a stereo tape system for his car, the latest garden or yard equipment, and visible additions to the house, such as a fancy television aerial, gates, ornate house signs, or other forms of exterior decoration. Inside, he will have a musical cocktail shaker and the latest radio-television-phonograph console with numerous speakers and dials.

It is actually possible to drive past a house and observe the low self-esteem of its occupant and whether or not he is a compulsive gadget collector. The gadget collector will have a mailbox and house numerals that are more decorative than utilitarian, and they will be unnecessarily prominent. There may be plastic or concrete statuary in the yard, and if there is a front porch or patio, it will be filled with furniture, pots, flowers, and hanging baskets. It is not unusual to see a picture window in which a large ornate table lamp is the center of attraction. The general appearance of the over-gadgeted house is one of overcrowding, both inside and outside.

Oral personalities will collect the latest in food appliances, pans, and dishes. They will get vicarious enjoyment out of thinking about the uses to which these culinary appliances can be put. The same applies to the drinker who likes to collect all kinds of bar gadgets.

Anal personalities do and say things that would be more appropriate for young children curious about their body functions. Harold had a strong anal character. He spent a lot of money buying silly gadgets which he thought were humorous. He had a bottle top that was the figure of a small boy urinating, which he liked to use when pouring drinks for friends, especially women. He had cups that were shaped like chamber pots. In his recreation room was a fake urinal used as an ashtray, and he had a musical holder for toilet paper in his bathroom. Persons who have retained this juvenile attitude toward sex and sexual matters will display it in their taste for gadgets. They will buy such items as ice cubes shaped like the nude bodies of women, nude and suggestive statuary or pictures, and glasses or other utensils that have sexual designs or are suggestive in nature. They may have fake telescopes or binoculars that contain photographs of nude women or scenes of sexual intercourse. There are gadgets marketed for those who want sexual stimulation. One company is doing a brisk business in manufacturing and selling life-size rubber inflatable women. You can also buy from the same company frilly underwear for your newest gadget!

Compulsive gadget-buying can result in living space so crammed with gadgets that there is not a square inch of free space left in which to put things. This is what has happened to Gail; she spends her lunch hours and Saturdays shopping, and she buys from mail-order catalogs. She "loves little things," and her apartment is crowded with gadgets of all kinds. A lonely woman who has never married, Gail misses the large family and small-town social life she was familiar with before she moved to the city. She is trying to fill up the emptiness and shut out the silence by purchasing things. In another sense she is buying gifts for the family she no longer has.

Betty had a somewhat similar problem. She was married, but her marriage was not a particularly happy one. Overweight and unhappy, Betty spent her spare time cooking, eating, and buying household gadgets. Her kitchen had the latest equipment and every device that appeared on the market, but she was still an unhappy woman. All the buying and all her kitchen activities were unsatisfactory substitutes for the love and affection she craved from her indifferent husband.

Some people buy gadgets because of laziness. Seeing a labor-saving device advertised, they rush to buy it. It gives them a sense of accomplishment —although they may never use it, they derive a psychic benefit from owning it. A man may have a garage filled with garden tools and a yard filled with weeds and uncut grass. He sits in the house watching baseball on television, content in the knowledge that he has the latest in yard equipment. And if the television commercial shows a new type of sprinkler or lawn mower, he will be one of the first to buy one.

Some people buy gadgets because they've retained a childish desire to have everything they see. Where they formerly whined for the shiny new toy, they now go through the same process for the shiny new gadget and will even sometimes pout in a most unbecoming nonadult way until they get what they think they want. Use or necessity does not enter into the picture; it is the wanting and the satisfying of the wanting that are important.

The desire to feel superior to others also influences gadget-buying. Some people insist on being the first in their social group to have a certain gadget, and the more exotic the gadget, the better they feel. If it later becomes easily available and is found in many homes, they lose interest in it and may find fault with it and refuse to use it anymore.

Gadgets for most people are the tangible evidence of their own material success, but they are also psychological evidence of an emotional state.

Gadgets are not necessities; they are wish-fulfillment items.

FURNISHINGS AND PERSONALITY

You can tell a great deal about a person when you enter his home. A jumble of colors and styles usually indicates emotional confusion on the part of the owner. A woman whose house exhibits jarring colors and styles, whose furnishings are a kind of *pasticcio*, may show the same confusion and fragmentation in her personal attitudes. An overcrowded house often indicates a compulsive talker who may also suffer from hypochondriasis.

People tend to project their feelings into their furniture and surroundings. A cold, unfriendly individual will have a cold, unfriendly house with uninviting and uncomfortable furniture. The "sterile" look in some homes reflects an emotional and sexual sterility in the owner. A house filled with antiques and mementos from the past reveals an owner disinclined to face the present and an overdependence upon family. The owner is not sure enough of his or her own tastes and so has to follow the tastes of generations before.

Constant redecorating and furniture rearrangement are expressions of unhappiness, dissatisfaction, and a strong desire to change the pattern of one's life. People with this compulsion are unable to change their lives, so they try to satisfy themselves by changing the furniture, drapes, or colors in their homes. They may also work off some of their anxiety in the physical effort of moving furniture.

"Madge is always redecorating her house. I'm

surprised she recognizes it from one week to another!" jokes a friend, but it is no joking matter to Madge, an unhappy and bitter woman. She is married to an alcoholic but lacks the courage to leave him, even though he mistreats her. Redecorating her house is symbolic of her desire to start a new life for herself.

A home that is casual and contains a minimum of gadgets is usually comfortable. The furniture is chosen for suitability and comfort; the colors blend well together and are warm in tone. Accessories are harmonious without being rigid in their conformity; styles may be mixed, but the overall effect is one of harmony. It is possible to walk into such a home and know instantly that its occupants are mature, well-adjusted individuals with love and concern for others. Their level of self-esteem is high enough that they do not have to depend on gadgets to reinforce their personalities.

Whose Garden Is It?

Gardens and yards of every size and description have continued to flourish and to indicate the personalities of their owners since the first biblical garden with its tree of life and tree of knowledge. Not only what you grow in your garden but how you take care of it and your attitude toward it can indicate specific personality traits.

Is your garden yours or your neighbors'? If you spend your time working there simply to impress others or to conform with neighborhood standards, you are showing shallowness and insincerity, characteristics that will also show up in other areas of your life. If you work in your yard when you would rather be doing something else but you are afraid of what the neighbors will say if you don't do as they do, you are weak and lacking in self-esteem. You do not value your own thoughts and opinions. You depend too much on the judgments and opinions of others. Your sense of values may be false, and you may place too much emphasis on status as against actual worth. Basically, you crave group approval.

A lawn or garden, like any other possession, can become a source of stress rather than enjoyment if the wrong values are attached to it or the wrong attitude develops around it. Sometimes the attitude toward the garden is a result of transference. A person who is actually worried about his family, his business, or his health will transfer those feelings of anxiety to his yard. When he expresses concern about whether or not his lawn will survive, he is really expressing a hidden fear of death, usually his own but perhaps the death of loved ones. And when he attacks the natural enemies in the garden—bugs, worms, blight, and other disasters—he is transferring his anger against the things that threaten him in his own life—sickness, inflation, violence, and accidents. Those things he cannot control, but the threats to his garden he can.

A husband and wife will sometimes transfer mutual hatred to safer ground—that is, the yard —and use it to attack and hurt each other emotionally. One man who knew his wife prized her flowers very highly deliberately ran the power lawn mower into the flower beds whenever he was angry with her. A woman refused to let her husband put up a hammock in their backyard because she felt that he did not do enough around the house. In another family the wife and husband, both of whom worked in the garden, would comment derisively on each other's gardening whenever friends came to visit. In some cases real rivalry can develop between a husband and wife over gardening, and here, too, it is a cover-up for rivalry in other areas of their life together. Competition has its place, but in a marriage competition of any form can be emotionally disastrous.

A yard covered with debris and a lawn filled with weeds may simply indicate laziness, but more often it indicates a flouting of one's neighbors. Today there are strict laws against dumping garbage in the yard, but you can express your hostility for your neighbors and your indifference to society by letting the weeds grow, by not picking up trash that blows into your yard, and by not raking your leaves. You may also let your children leave their toys or bicycles lying in the yard, and in some neighborhoods it is not uncommon to see an old car rusting away in a side yard or driveway. These are all ways of expressing contempt and dislike for others. If you do this, you probably do it in other areas of your life such as dressing inappropriately, smoking when smoking is prohibited, and breaking minor rules such as litter and traffic regulations. The individual who acts this way, who enjoys putting people down any way that he can, is actually a coward. He wouldn't have the nerve to go over to his neighbor and tell him what he thinks of him, but he does let his weeds grow, knowing that this will affront the neighbor who is particular about his own lawn. The person with a litter-filled yard is an exhibitionist who has never grown up, who still gets pleasure out of safely defying authority of all kinds, including the authority of public opinion.

Gardens are an extension of our personalities, limited only by our imaginations. They can help us to express what measure of creativity we have within us. For most people an interest in gardening shows an interest in exterior things and some measure of concern for the world around them.

YOU AND YOUR ENVIRONMENT

Your environment should not be unchangeable or static; it should be pliable in order to be truly viable. An environment should reflect your continual growth capabilities—and what you lived with ten years ago may not be what you should be surrounded with now. It is important that your environment be one that both satisfies you and stimulates you. It is your own small world, and your success, happiness, and adjustment patterns in the larger world to which you belong will often be determined to a great extent by your ability to cope with your immediate environment and its problems.

6

What Do You Want to Be
When You Grow Up?

THE RIGHT JOB

Freedom of choice in picking a job or profession exists today as never before in history. Vocational counseling and guidance are a twentieth-century phenomenon. However, despite the many guidance tests now available, most people continue to select their lifework on a purely emotional basis or on the basis of chance. Getting the right person in the right job was probably easier during the period of the medieval guilds. Not only were there fewer choices, hence fewer causes for dissatisfaction, but there was a strong body of tradition surrounding each occupation which gave it a force and an importance that helped the individual worker to adjust to his lifework. He could have pride in the profession he chose because after serving an apprenticeship he could feel that he was worthy of his particular craft whether it was metalwork or law. Apprenticeship was thus a form of vocational counseling, and it also gave the apprentice a vital sense of continuity with the past. The widespread system of apprenticeships, which was the lifeblood of the guilds, failed in time because it was too rigid and was overcome by the proliferation of new trades and the rise of individual capitalism.

Today individuals are no longer bound by guild and trade rules when they select their occupation, but their success in making the right choice is no more guaranteed than it was under the old system. In fact, some probably make poorer choices than they would if they had some firm direction. Many times the reasons for choosing a certain profession are deeply buried in the unconscious. In any case, the individual who makes a personal choice reveals something about his personality and psychological makeup.

MOTIVATIONS IN OCCUPATIONAL CHOICES

The profession or occupation you are in tells the world what you are, but the reasons you chose that particular profession or job tell why you are the way you are. In fact, your choice of profession or job may tell more about the kind of person you are than you realize or care to have known.

In the most basic sense you select your lifework simply because you have to do some kind of work in order to take care of basic economic necessities. The degree to which an occupation satisfies those needs often determines its popularity and accounts for the satisfaction an individual receives from it. In most cases, however, the basic reason is not the only one. There are other factors that motivate you in making your choices. Understanding the emotional and psychological reasons for your job choice may help you to understand yourself better. When you select an occupation, you are also choosing a future lifestyle. It is your occupation and how well you succeed in it that determine your social status, the kind of friends you will have, your leisure-time activities, and sometimes even the kind of marriage partner you will attract.

Some people pick their occupations to please their parents. In doing this they become extensions of their parents' egos. This will often come about when a parent is disappointed in his own occupation or the occupation of the spouse. As one mother told me, "I don't care what my son does, but it has to be in one of the professions. I know what a struggle we've had because my husband did not finish college and go into some profession. Besides that, he will have a better place in society than we were able to have, and he can make a better marriage." She would have denied that she was being materialistic and selfish, insisting that she was only being practical and looking after her son's welfare. She would not have wanted to face the fact that her own disappointment with her husband and her married life in terms of its lack of social and economic fulfillment contributed to her decision. Many parents attempt to make a second life for themselves through their children, and nowhere is this more quickly shown than when they dictate their occupational choices. And if the choice of the parents does not coincide with the children's own desires, the results can be disastrous.

Ruth had severe headaches for which no organic cause could be found, so her family doctor suggested that she consult a psychiatrist. When

I saw Ruth, she was thin and suffered from sleeplessness because of her headaches. Although she insisted that she had no problems other than her physical condition, analysis revealed that there was a struggle going on between Ruth and her mother. Ruth's mother had always wanted to be a nurse, but the combination of a lack of the right opportunity and an early marriage had kept her from entering that profession. Now she was insisting that Ruth become a nurse, although Ruth wanted to study fashion design, a career for which she had an aptitude. It was the constant bickering over this subject that was causing Ruth's headaches. She was subconsciously looking for a way out of the situation without hurting her mother. "I keep telling my mother that I'm not strong enough to be a nurse. These headaches prove that!"

Ruth's mother was trying to get her second chance through her daughter, and it looked as if she was going to suffer another case of frustration. Fortunately, a solution was found that pleased both of them, ended their family quarrel, and raised their self-esteem. Ruth's mother was asked to investigate the possibility of becoming a practical nurse while she let her daughter go ahead and become a fashion designer. Both mother and daughter went to school. Ruth, no longer suffering from headaches, is now a dress designer and fashion coordinator for a large store, her mother is a licensed practical nurse in the city hospital.

Letting your parents choose your occupation or profession indicates a lack of self-confidence. You have little or no faith in your own judgment. You probably also let them decide on other major issues in your life, such as whom you should marry. You may be a timid "model" child, even as an adult afraid to question authority. You want to be told what to do. You will even allow yourself to be pushed into an occupation you don't like because you are afraid to express what little individuality you possess. In many respects you are a carbon copy of your father or mother. This pleases them but may give you ulcers, nervous indigestion, back pains, and other psychosomatic ills.

You may choose your profession reflexively in that you automatically follow the same profession as your father and perhaps his father before him. This, like any other choice not based on individual preference or ability, can lead to serious emotional trouble. Anyone who permits himself to be directed into the family business or profession when he is not interested in it is going to have an unhappy life. As a personality he will always live in the shadow of his father. By showing his willingness to follow a directive that does not appeal to him he is showing a lack of self-esteem and displaying a weakness of character that will be a handicap to him all his life. His ability to make good, sound business decisions will also be impaired.

"I became a lawyer because it was expected of me," explained one patient. "I knew my father expected it of me because our family law firm has been in operation for over eighty years. Even as a child I was told that someday I would join my father in the firm just as he had joined his father. I wanted to be an architect, but I didn't have the courage to say so. I regret it now, but it is too late. I used to wish that I had a brother who could have taken my place, but I was an only child. Now I see that my father is pressuring my son to study law, but he wants to become a musician. I hope that I can stick to my guns and let my son decide for himself in a way I never could."

The speaker was only moderately successful in his law practice and very unsuccessful as a person. His marriage was an unhappy one, and he himself was suffering from depression and anxiety. The truth was that he despised himself as a person, and this had affected his whole life.

Parents may directly or indirectly lead their children to select a prestige occupation in order to enhance their own personalities or positions in society and add to the family wealth and name. "My son, the doctor" is really not a joke but a reality of family life. The idea of a prestige occupation is always held up as desirable to young people in disadvantaged or even moderate circumstances, but too often it is realistically impossible for them to sustain their interest and motivations long enough to reach that occupational status. Some do make it, however, because they see their work as the only means of extricating themselves from lives and conditions that have become intolerable to them.

Prestige is a common motivation for selecting a profession or occupation. It is a strong motivation, since it leads to a determination to strive and work toward the top. A person so motivated may be very single-minded with all the emphasis on his career. He may be a brilliant scientist but a dull conversationalist or a highly successful industrialist but a weak father and family man.

If you have chosen your career purely on the motivation of prestige, you may be ruthless in your climb toward success. Persons such as yourself are often willing to sacrifice family life, friendships, and even a happy marriage in order to achieve desired career goals.

Laziness can actually be a motivating force in selecting a career. The individual who does not want to work but feels forced by social and family pressures to take a job will look for one that is undemanding. He will often select the first job he hears about, whether or not it is suitable, because he is too lazy to look for another one. Prestige, advancement, and salary rarely interest the lazy person. He is interested only in fulfilling the conventional requirements of his social and family group mores—that he have a job.

Some people are motivated to select a career on the basis of economic security only. They willingly give up dreams of a more adventurous life in order to have a steady job with a secure future. Like the lazy person, advancement and prestige do not interest them, but the prospect of a regular salary does. As a result, they are sometimes vaguely dissatisfied with themselves and their lives. They may have secret doubts as to the ultimate wisdom of their career choices.

"I became a librarian because it was steady work, and although I've enjoyed it, in a way I feel as if I missed something," said Anna.

"Electricians get good wages, so I decided I would take that up," explained Donald. "I've made a good living, and I and my family are very comfortable. However, sometimes I have this nagging sensation that life could have been more interesting and more fun if I had looked for something besides economic security when I picked a career."

Parental pressure, prestige, laziness, and economic security are all everyday reasons for making occupational choices. But in addition, there are other motivations that are not so obvious and are psychological in nature.

CHILDHOOD FANTASIES AND ADULT CAREER CHOICES

The fantasies, impulses, and drives of childhood are frequently sublimated and converted into useful social occupations in adulthood. Through playing, toys, and daydreams children act out their fantasies and impulses. Like actors trying out for parts, they put on various faces and try out gestures. All this play action is a part of the growing-up process, and as a part of this process children learn what impulses and what drives are socially acceptable and which ones have to be repressed or changed. It can thus lead to or influence the choice of an occupation.

A boy who is sadistic and cruel in his childhood play may later sublimate these impulses into a humanitarian occupation. As a boy he may have found pleasure in pulling the wings off flies; as an adult he may become a surgeon. In a sense he is still pulling wings off flies, but now it is for a socially acceptable purpose. Other doctors, nurses, and medical workers had childhood fantasies of rescuing people. As adults they carry out this fantasy theme in a practical and useful way.

A little girl who is bossy and likes to tell other children what to do may become a teacher of small children where her authority is accepted without question.

Lawyers are frequently individuals who as

children felt imposed upon by adults, particularly their parents, or felt that they were unfairly treated by authority figures. They therefore spend their lives defending people who are being unjustly treated. In this way they are satisfying their childhood desire to get justice for themselves.

Some children who are frequently punished and harassed have fantasies in which they get even with their parents or other adults. Since these have to remain fantasies and the revenge is never accomplished, the impulse is still present when they reach adulthood. To satisfy it they may take up an occupation in which they can safely act out those sublimated fantasies. They may become policemen when they grow up. Even though they may not realize it when they tell other people to "Move along," in their unconscious thinking they are ordering their parents around as they never could when they were children.

Besides power fantasies, children often have fantasies of food and wealth that later influence their choice of an occupation. They imagine themselves as being able to satify all their desires, as having unlimited amounts of money. The child who has daydreams of this nature will often become a ruthless and aggressive leader in whatever profession he chooses.

Food and want played a role in the success of the owner of a chain of grocery stores. As he explained it to me, "When I was a child, my family was very poor, and often we went hungry. I was always conscious that there was not enough food to go around for all of us. I used to dream of having a grocery store of my own and being able to have whatever I wanted. When I grew up, I decided to make that dream come true. I started out clerking in a grocery store, and later I bought a store, then another one and another until I owned a chain of groceries."

Aggressive children will usually adopt aggressive adult occupations. They will choose careers in law enforcement, sports, military service, or in other fields that permit them to discharge their aggressive drives physically. One young man who had been trained as an accountant gave it up and became a dock worker because he could not control his aggressive impulses in a sedentary job. "It seemed as if anger would just accumulate inside over nothing at all, and suddenly it would boil over and then I'd be in real trouble at work and at home! When I changed to a job that kept me physically busy, it seemed to take care of the anger I used to have. My wife says I'm much easier to get along with these days." Another man who was a butcher admitted that he had taken up his occupation because it satisfied his aggressive impulses.

PERSONALITY TYPES AND OCCUPATIONS

When we look at society and the various kinds of jobs and professions that are daily being carried out, we are looking at an externalization of man's unconscious personality structure. In this sense we all live in a dream world, for although we conceive of ourselves as having real jobs and doing real things, we are actually acting out unconscious wishes and fantasies in the external world. We may also be acting out fears and guilts that may be so firmly embedded in our unconscious that we do not realize the extent to which they influence our actions.

Guilt plays a very prominent part in career selection. The guilty person may try to use his or her career in an attempt to cover up the feelings that produce the guilt or in an effort to expiate that guilt. It is not unusual to find that the stern moralist is also suffering from difficulty in coping with strong sexual desire. Because of this, he feels that all people have the same problem and that the safest solution is to try to eliminate the pursuit and enjoyment of sex.

A patient who suffered from anxiety finally admitted that she had sexual fantasies and impulses that disturbed her. She had come from a family that had a strictly enforced code of morality. "I was always curious about sexual matters and about such things as nakedness, but when I asked my mother, I was told that only a wicked and abnormal person would be interested in such things. As a result, I grew up without having my curiosity satisfied and feeling guilty because I was interested in knowing more about such things. I decided to become a nurse because I knew that at least that way I could learn about the human body and sex functions. Only now I find that I get a thrill out of seeing a naked body, and I know that this is wrong."

The same guilt that had led her into choosing nursing as a profession was making her sick. With treatment she was able to achieve a more mature attitude toward sexual matters.

The person who is essentially greedy and wants everything for himself may go into social-service work because of his guilt over his greed. As a child he may have been reprimanded and perhaps even punished by his parents for being selfish; therefore, as an adult he feels the constant necessity to prove that he is really not selfish, even though he may actually still be selfish and greedy. Any social-service or religious occupation may attract people who feel the need to show off their good qualities and at the same time have control over the lives of others. Such occupations are ego boosters in that they elicit praise from others and at the same time convey a means of exercising authority over other people.

The anal person who as a child gained his pleasure from the expulsion of feces—from being praised by his mother for his cooperation in being trained—is ambitious and confident. He will always be basically a "giver" and will enjoy working in a job where he can give some service or product to other people. On the other hand, however, we more often think of the anal personality as one that is characterized by frugality, obstinacy, and orderliness. All these characteristics can be directly traced to the child's early toilet-training period. The frugal adult was the child who enjoyed retention rather than expulsion. As an adult he becomes a hoarder or a miser. He does well as a museum curator or a librarian or in a similar custodial or collecting-type position. Obstinacy is related to the child's rebellion against his mother's commands to have his defecation periods when and where she decided. This child may become the adult who continues through life unhappy and at odds with all forms of authority. He usually has a chip on his shoulder and is easily irritated at orders or commands. In the work world he rarely suceeds because he is unwilling to accept direction and as a result may become a chronic job hopper. This type of person does best if he can work by himself in a job that does not require him to deal directly with others. He often does well as a craftsman working by himself. The orderly adult is usually also very punctual and anxious to do the right thing, just as he was anxious to please his mother by being clean and obeying her toilet-training commands. As an adult he is nonaggressive and timid in occupations; he does well in accounting, bookkeeping, clerking, or any position in which he is required to take care of things. He is a "by the rules" person and quite inflexible in his ideas and habits. The anal personality does well and feels comfortable in banking. The individual who suffered from chronic diarrhea as a child because of his anxiety over pleasing his mother will still have this impulse to give as an adult and to give in order to be loved. He will enjoy being the bank officer who gives loans and home mortgages to people. On the other hand the man who did not want to give up his feces as a child will be more cautious and conservative in his banking operations and will derive pleasure from saying No to people and from foreclosing on mortgages.

The oral personality comes from that stage in a child's development when his whole life is concentrated on the pleasures of his mouth, such as sucking and eating. Adults who remain psychologically oriented at this stage will look for occupations that continue to satisfy their oral needs. They may enjoy work as chefs, bakers, waiters, or waitresses or open their own restaurants. Because talkativeness is another expression of the oral character, they may become teachers, radio or television announcers, salesmen, or lecturers. One of the best combinations would probably be a salesman of a food product.

The narcissistic personality is one of persistent emotional immaturity. However, such an individual can often succeed in his lifework if he chooses an occupation that permits him to satisfy his narcissistic desires. He does well as an actor, an artist, a writer, or a musician—any occupation he can interpret as being an extension of his own personality and one in which he can gain satisfaction from the applause and admiration of others.

Fear of death can be a factor in choosing a career and is allied in many persons to the rescue fantasy. The person who feared the dark as a child and as an adult fears death may try to compensate for that fear by engaging in work that prolongs life. Such diverse occupations as lifeguard, doctor, and research scientist will attract this personality. A doctor who had received acclaim for his work in pinpointing the possible causes of some well-known diseases told me that he really felt that he shouldn't be given so much praise and credit, for, he frankly admitted, it was his desire to escape death that kept him interested in medical research.

THE OTHER SIDE OF SUCCESS

There have been many instances of individuals who work hard, do well, receive coveted promotions, and then perform so badly that they are later dismissed or demoted. There are psychologi-

cal reasons for this kind of failure, this breakdown in either personality reactions or efficiency.
Most of the patients I have treated who have
work-related problems have had these emotional
and mental difficulties because they have succeeded, not because they have failed! One of
Sigmund Freud's famous cases was that of a
judge who, when he received an appointment to
the highest court in the land, a position he had
long desired, suffered a mental collapse. The
reason for his and other, similar breakdowns is
that such people have been acting out their
dream lives and childhood fantasies, and when
suddenly the desired goal is reached, the dream
ends, and they find themselves unable to
function. Some people do not have this problem
because as fast as they reach one goal, they re-
place it with another, and if they can manage to
keep from running out of goals, they can keep
emotionally solvent.

Reaching the top can also be disastrous psychologically when that achievement is equated
with surpassing and destroying the father. This
is an emotional problem related to the superego.
It is common enough to inhibit some people from
ever achieving success or from being able to
enjoy that success. Some women also have a problem if they feel guilty about surpassing their
mothers. One woman whom I treated for a nervous breakdown was a successful department-
store executive, whose success had triggered a
series of unpleasant family episodes in which her
mother blamed her for not following in her foot-
steps by marrying and having a family. The
mother felt that my patient was deliberately tak-

ing a course of action to spite her and had created feelings of guilt in her daughter.

THE MYTH OF DISCOVERY AND OTHER ADULT FANTASIES

One part of the American dream has always been the "discovery" theme—talented unknown who is "discovered" and immediately becomes an overnight success, a person of wealth, and a heroic figure. It is the old Cinderella story in modern guise. The theme has appeared in songs ("I Found a Million-Dollar Baby in a Five-and-Ten-Cent Store") and in countless plays, movies, and books. It is a theory that has become part of modern mythology, and strangely enough, it has happened just often enough to lend credibility to the theory. However, for every true case of discovery there are thousands who languish "undiscovered," unhappy, and forever unknown. The myth serves its purpose, however, because it is just such fantasies of future glory that help many lower-echelon workers stay happy. This phenomenon is not confined to the young beginner, for in any work force you can find the middle-aged or older worker who is still waiting for that "big break."

The secretary who has seen enough movies and television shows to believe that someday "Mr. Right" will come along and notice her will be content with her position, at least for a time. At last she may do as her mother did before her and settle for the boy next door or down the street. With the frequent examples of "instant" stardom in television and rock music the aspiring young singer works happily at the drive-in, confidently hoping his next customer will be a producer or an agent looking for new talent.

Few people feel really involved in their work or satisfied by it because they have chosen it on the basis of unconscious motivations which stem from childhood fantasies. They are unable to give their full attention to their jobs because either they dislike what they are doing or it cannot hold their interest. That is why many workers "goof off" by wasting time in unnecessary trips to the restroom, horseplay, visiting with fellow employees, and thinking up ways to extend the coffee break. Actually most workers expend more energy trying to look busy than doing their assigned work.

IDENTIFICATION AND OCCUPATIONAL CHOICES

Identification is a combination of how we see ourselves, how we accept the way others see us, and our level of self-esteem. It can be a factor in the development of a well-integrated personality, or it can be the cause of emotional problems. It influences attitudes and behavior and plays a definite role in the selection of an occupation.

Children who are constantly put down by their parents and other adults grow up to find they are unable to accept themselves at full value. They have accepted the picture of themselves as incompetent. They identify with failure and have low self-esteem. As adults they tend to take jobs that are beneath them, and they do not attempt to develop their abilities. Working at low-level jobs serves to reinforce their poor opinion of themselves and helps to prove their own unworthiness.

Some people identify so strongly with the family unit and its security that they have to perpetuate that situation at all costs. We call this the eternal family syndrome, and it is seen on the one hand in the man or woman who remains a college student all or most of his life and on the other in the individual who seeks the safety of a minor job in civil service or in some large corporation. Such a person is afraid of the aggressive competition in higher jobs and smaller companies and wants the security of a pseudo-family situation. In a sense this individual has never left home. He wants the security and authority of parents and no personal responsibility or necessity to make decisions. In a typical case a man may go to college from home and then into a company job so that he is never left on his own. His life is regulated by those who are in charge of his time.

"I like working for the X company," Robert explained. "You know, they really take care of their people. We have a dandy recreation program, social events, a good hospital plan, and a pension system that is better than any other I've heard of, and now they are starting a travel program so that we can take trips at cost with other company employees. Next year I'm taking my family to Mexico on a company-sponsored tour."

For Robert the company picnic took the place of a family reunion, and the company with its comprehensive welfare and social programs took care of all his possible needs. He felt like a member of a large, thoughtful family, and as long as he continued to work for the X company, he would never be alone in the world. As he proudly pointed out, even after retirement he would still be considered a member of the company family and could use the recreational facilities of the company clubhouse and attend the company social functions. The X company was fulfilling Robert's dream and his needed identification, for he felt empty unless he was allowed to be a part of some group. The best military personnel are those who deliberately seek out the military life because of its encompassing control of the individual's lifestyle. The longing for security, the desire to avoid personal responsibility, and the willingness to follow orders without question make for an ideal member of any kind of military force. The army, navy, or air force becomes, like the large corporation, the surrogate parent, or "Big Daddy."

Being happy in and fulfilled through your work is one of the marks of the well-integrated, mature personality. Trying to cope with the job or profession that is not right for you can be as painful and awkward a procedure as wearing shoes that do not fit. You don't feel at ease, and you show it to the world. You can gain insight into your personality needs by analyzing your reasons for choosing your lifework, and you can decide for yourself why you are what you are in terms of your occupation. What part did sublimation play in your choice? Did you make your own choice, or did your family influence you? What part does fantasy play in your present work, and is it keeping you from realizing your true capabilities?

In general, you can remember some of these

guidelines about what career choices indicate about personality: Timid people generally choose quiet, unobtrusive occupations. They may become librarians, clerical workers, technicians, civil-service workers, or workers in a large company. They look for positions that are not controversial. Teaching was formerly a favorite choice of timid people because it had a built-in advantage—respect from students and the community. This has all changed with the new aggressiveness of the modern student, and the timid now flee from teaching as vigorously as they once flocked to it.

Aggressive people look for jobs that will let them express that aggressiveness in acceptable ways. They become soldiers, truck drivers, professional athletes, salesmen, or dock or construction workers. Very closely allied to them in temperament are the people who also want adventure. They look for satisfaction in military life, law enforcement, positions that require travel, high-rise construction work, bridge-building, or mining. Power, plus an element of danger, will be the deciding factor in some occupational choices, such as the professional soldier, the policeman, or the fireman.

Those who have dreams of glory in which they are looked up to by other people will choose high personality-impact occupations. They may become doctors, religious leaders, politicians, lawyers, or judges. Also high on their list of preferred professions will be those in the art and entertainment fields.

Family- and group-oriented persons satisfy their need to be surrounded by others by becoming social workers, teachers, nurses, or prison guards. They not only like to be a part of a closed family-type circle but want others to be dependent upon them.

These are only some of the many possible interpretations of occupation choices, and it is for you to decipher the correct interpretation of your own choice. The important thing is your attitude toward your job or profession and the kind of satisfaction that you are getting from it. You may find that you have made a wrong choice and that now with your knowledge of what psychological factors go into your choice you can make a second and a wiser choice.

7

What Do You Do for Fun?

A PSYCHOLOGICAL LOOK AT LEISURE

For centuries the average man worked six days
a week from sunup to sundown. Work was considered not only necessary but a virtue, at least
for the laboring classes, and the only time off
was a day of rest sanctioned by religion. It was
believed that "six days shalt thou labour and do
all thy work: But the seventh day . . . thou shalt
not do any work." It was not until the seventeenth
century that leisure became a part of the vocabu-
lary, if not a part of the lives of ordinary citizens.
The educated and upper classes had leisure time
which they spent in activities such as hunting,
fishing, reading, writing, and various sports. The
working classes still worked long hours, but the
notion of having free time was beginning to take
hold. It was during this period that Sir William
Temple, the English essayist and diplomat,
wrote: "The desire of leisure is much more natural than of business and care." By the mid-
nineteenth century reformers were beginning to

press for a shorter workweek and a shorter work-day. But the benefits of free time were not made available to all people in this country until almost the middle of the twentieth century. Interestingly enough, the latest trend is to lengthen the work-day to ten hours but shorten the workweek to four days. Both management and labor like the new four-day week and feel that it offers advantages that were not possible under the old scheme of five eight-hour days in which there was often, especially at certain seasons, a high rate of absenteeism. The four-day week gives each worker a three-day bloc of time, which can be used for leisure activities. Wherever the four-day workweek has been adopted there have been noticeable changes in life-style patterns. More persons report being able to engage in family activities such as camping, boating, and sight-seeing. There has been more attendance at sports events and more participation in club and civic groups. Many persons have indicated that as a result of the shorter workweek they plan to take courses, develop their hobbies, or do other things for self-improvement. There are also a significant number of people who see the shorter week as an opportunity to have more time in which to loaf and do nothing.

There will be problems in connection with the four-day work-week just as there will be great benefits, and the problems will be emotional and psychological in nature. Many people are simply not able to handle that much leisure time. They can't handle the hours they now have, and in some cases it is because they do not understand what leisure should do for them and what it can mean in terms of personal renewal and enrichment.

Leisure is another way in which we express our hidden personality characteristics, and it is not only what we do in our leisure time that reveals our personality, but our attitude toward leisure as well. Psychologically, leisure is important. It is a time when the individual can freely express many of his needs and desires. It is a change of pace both physically and emotionally. Yet, despite the obvious benefits, some people cannot use their leisure, and others misuse it.

Enjoying Your Free Time

Today you have longer vacations, more holidays, sometimes shorter workweeks, and fewer home responsibilities. You don't have to hunt for your food, haul water, chop wood, or spend hours preparing meals. For long hours you are free— free to do whatever you choose, go wherever you want. You have a multitude of activities to choose from when deciding what to do with your free time. Are you able to really enjoy your leisure? Are you able to relax? If you aren't, you may be cheating yourself.

The person who can't relax doesn't have any fun with his leisure hours; in fact, all that free time is disturbing to him. This tense, nervous personality is caused by feelings of insecurity. Such a person fears leisure because he feels exposed without the ready-made protection of work activities. He has low self-esteem, a shallow personality, and little self-confidence in areas of his life other than his work.

Thornton was a good worker who often worked overtime and always volunteered to do extra things around the plant; he refused to take part, however, in any group social activities. He was noted less for his work than for his unwillingness to attend the company picnic, parties, and special social events. Younger employees characterized him as an "old grouch," but the truth was that Thornton was afraid of social gatherings. He felt inadequate and inept, so he avoided people. Thornton had become socially timid when he was laughed at during adolescence for being clumsy. In his own mind Thornton still saw himself as a clumsy and socially inadequate person. When he worked, he felt adequate and in command of himself and the situation. He could not stand leisure because it brought him face to face with his poor self-image. Insecure people are always on the sidelines of any activity, declining to participate. "I just want to watch" is a favorite expression of theirs. Usually such people suffer doubly because not only do they feel inadequate but they also really want to be able to take part in the activity.

Miranda came for consultation because of increasing sleeplessness which was making her nervous and tired. When asked about her social activities, Miranda reeled off an impressive list —bowling, dancing, miniature golf, and other things. But later, Miranda admitted that although she accompanied her friends to these activities, she herself did not actually take part. As she explained, "I'd only make a fool of myself in front of people, and I couldn't stand that. I'd just die if I had to get up in front of the others and do things. Besides, I'm just too nervous to do things, and I get tired so easily. My friends all understand this, and they don't expect me to do things that I can't do."

She was not only extremely self-conscious but very insecure. Her inability to relax was slowly eroding her physical health. She had to be taught the meaning of self-worth and to understand that her inability to relax and have fun meant that she had a poor opinion of herself. She had fooled herself and others into believing that she was too nervous and weak to do the things that other people were doing. The only "tonic" Miranda needed to be able to let go and have a good time was to build up her self-esteem. When she did that, she was able to take part in all kinds of group social activities.

Feeling guilty when you take time out for some leisure fun shows a lack of maturity. This feeling of guilt comes from some unresolved traumatic childhood experience. If you were raised in a home where the importance of work and devotion to duty were stressed, you will not be able to relax as an adult. You will become one of those adults to whom leisure is a waste of time. If you can't enjoy your leisure time because you feel guilty, you are behaving both foolishly and immaturely. You are still acting like a child. You are carrying out the orders and suggestions given to you as a child instead of taking your place as an adult. In many other ways you have no doubt freed yourself from the strict regulations of your childhood, but with regard to your leisure time you have been unable to get away.

Being able to relax and enjoy your leisure time shows that you are emotionally balanced with a happy personality and good positive personality characteristics. Using your leisure time in a creative and pleasant way shows a realistic adaptation to life. You understand the reasons leisure is important, and you allow for a reasonable amount of your time to be spent in relaxation by developing a work-play rhythm in your life.

AGGRESSION AND LEISURE

Aggression as an id impulse is constantly seeking for some means of expression, and leisure furnishes one area into which raw aggressive drives can be channeled. In fact, the times of recreation are the only times in which many people can discharge their aggression. One of the ways this is done is by allowing someone else to perform aggressively while you watch; the second way is to perform some aggressive but acceptable act yourself.

Most sports satisfy the need for aggression outlets. In particular, boxing, wrestling, football, hockey, basketball, and baseball all satisfy this need for aggression relief. Obviously the more aggression present in an individual, the more needed relief will be obtained from violent sports. One man will find that his aggressive drives are fulfilled by going out and hitting a golf ball, but another man will need to work out his aggressive impulses by watching a football game. Many times the aggressive drives are so repressed that on the surface the individual will be exceedingly calm and even-tempered, yet inside he or she may have a seething mass of aggressive and hostile impulses. Undischarged, those impulses can result in ulcers, headaches, insomnia, and other psychosomatic ills. But if the impulses are permitted discharge through some permissible activity, the individual is able to keep his outward calmness and his health. This explains why the mildest of men and the gentlest of women may get great relief from tension by attending or watching on television certain violent games. In addition to the vicarious satisfaction of watching the aggressive violence, there are the extra dividends of clapping, yelling, cheering, jumping up and down, and waving of arms. Anyone who has ever listened to the fans at a football, baseball, or other game knows how aggressive and even at times abusive the yelling can become.

For some people, watching a game is not enough activity to satisfy their aggressive drives, and they feel the need to participate themselves in some kind of recreation. The kind they select will depend upon the intensity of their aggressive drives. If it is not too strong, they will be satisfied with a sport such as bowling, in which each time they bowl and knock pins down, they lose some of their aggression. However, if their feelings are strong and demanding, they will instinctively seek out some more violent sport, one in which there is body contact, competition, and the use of a large amount of physical energy. Boxing is very popular with such people, as are handball and tennis. Fencing is one leisure-time sport that fulfills the requirements of many aggressive people. It is a sport and an art that is highly competitive and uses a great deal of physical energy as well as demanding quick thinking and mental calculations from the participants. Although fencing is no longer a means of settling disputes, it is still a challenging game of skill; it may not end in bloodshed, but it simulates the actions leading up to the final blow and thus satisfies some very primitive aggressive impulses. Bullfighting caters to those impulses on a larger scale. Just as in fencing but with a final difference of the actual kill, there are the ageless patterns of pursuit, offense-defense actions, wounding (or capturing), and the kill.

Competition is natural, and you should enjoy taking part in some recreation in which competition is a factor. You may, however, be cheating yourself out of your needed relaxation if you place too much emphasis on competition. If recreation means only competition to you, you are not really having fun.

On the other side of aggression there is the individual who absolutely refuses to take part in any sport because of a fear of getting hurt. This fear may be concealed so that the person does not say, "I am afraid," but rather, "I am too tired," or "I'm just not interested." Fear of injury can usually be traced to a childhood experience or an accident connected with sports that has left a traumatic scar. Or overly protective parents may have forbidden participation in competitive sports, and that prohibition is still psychologically in effect. Fear of sports can also conceal a fear of death itself. The individual does not want to engage in any type of activity that could bring him into physical danger. This person also fears diseases and infections and clings to a life that is safe but basically dull.

Fear combined with a desire to overcome that fear may lead some persons to seek out highly competitive and aggressive sports. This is often true during adolescence when there is a strong desire to prove masculinity and the right to the privileges of manhood. This can lead to reckless and foolhardy conduct as when a young boy will try to perform in sports what is physically impossible for him to do.

REGRESSION, GREED, SELF-IMAGE, AND LEISURE

Regression is a form of return to an early, less mature state of behavior. It is a primitive reaction that enables you to play, to laugh, and to express yourself and your emotions directly and without thinking of what kind of an impression you are making on others. This regression is healthy, and those who are unable to regress have dull, rigid personalities. On the other hand the person who cannot stop his regressive tendencies when the time for them is over becomes merely obnoxious and silly. There are times when you should act silly, lose your compulsion to be firm and dignified, and let yourself relax. Many times a person of importance and dignity will be persuaded to lose himself in a game or social situation and is later heard to remark, "I haven't had so much fun in years!" If you can lose yourself in a game or in watching some sport, you have a flexible, warm personality. You get fun out of life, and you are fun for other people to be with. As a rule you have friends of all ages because you are considered to be a good sport. People like to invite you to come to their parties and other social functions.

If you have trouble in regressing to a relaxing level, it may be because of your childhood. Your parents may have been so emphatic in cautioning you not to act foolish that you have been conditioned to avoid any semblance of relaxed behavior. Again it is important for you to realize that as an adult you can tell yourself what to do, and one of the things you should learn to do is to make a fun time out of your leisure hours.

Regressive leisure-time activities usually include some form of change from your daily routines. This change can be very beneficial in terms of renewing your emotional strength. The busy executive who leaves his air-conditioned office and home to go on a fishing trip in the wilds, unconcerned about comforts and cleanliness, is making the right use of regression.

Greed as a personality characteristic shows up in all of an individual's activities, including those connected with his leisure time. Greed finds a natural outlet in the collecting of objects. The individual may say that he is collecting stamps, matchbook covers, or bottles, but the particular type of object being collected does not really matter; it is the satisfying of the acquisitive instinct. This type of personality is usually the anal type, and he wishes not only to accumulate as much as possible but to then hang on to it. He wants to have the most complete collection, the biggest collection, or the best collection.

Your self-image influences the way you spend your leisure time. Just as the aggressive person enjoys watching or participating in sports, so the person whose self-image is one of timidity may avoid spending his leisure time with other people and instead spend it by himself listening to music, reading books, or pursuing a hobby that he can do by himself.

The individual whose self-image is one of passive adaption will not be able to plan his leisure activities. He will sit around waiting for something to happen or for someone else to suggest some form of activity. He lacks initiative, and in leisure as in all other areas of his life he needs and wants constant direction and some form of supervision. This is the adult who as a child continually whined, "I don't know what to do!" and "What should I do now?" As an adult he wastes time because he doesn't know how to handle unscheduled hours.

Charles makes plans for his weekends, and holidays, but he never carries them out. He is a worrier and a poor planner, and the combination means lost hours and frustration. On a recent typical weekend Charles planned on going fishing, but he never made it to the lake. He was delayed first because he had to get his equipment ready and then he tried unsuccessfully to find a friend to go along. After that he couldn't decide what time he should leave, and he questioned whether or not the weather would be suitable. He finally did not get away at all, and the results were feelings of anger and irritation. Charles was angry at the world in general, but he really should have been angry with himself.

If you have a conception of yourself as a person of intellectual attainments when this is not true, you will be unhappy trying to keep up an impossible level of achievement. Rick actually preferred spectator sports, but to please his fiancée, he persuaded himself that he enjoyed more intellectual activities in his leisure time. He signed up for courses at the local college and attended concerts and lectures, but he eventually became quite morose. His unhappiness translated into irritation, and the engagement was broken as a result. Later, when Rick learned to accept his real self-image, he not only enjoyed his leisure time pursuing his real interests but was able to find a girl who shared them. There is nothing wrong in preferring rock music to opera or vice versa. It is your attitude and your degree of honesty about your leisure-time pursuits that are important.

The oral personality will probably choose a hobby such as gourmet cooking, collecting recipes, or visiting famous restaurants. He may also get satisfaction out of gardening as a hobby, especially vegetable gardening, since from ground to table is only a short distance.

Whatever your self-image, it is reflected in your hobbies and spare-time activities. If you think of yourself as creative, you will do creative things even if you lack natural talent. You may have to substitute paint-by-number kits for original works of art, but you will be satisfying your self-image as a creative person.

Childhood fantasies can become part of your self-image and find an outlet in your choice of leisure activities. The man who as a child saw himself growing up to be a big-league baseball player can satisfy that fantasy by playing baseball with his hometown or company team. The cheers of his neighbors and friends will be as sweet to him as he once imagined the cheers would be in a big stadium. The woman who dreamed of becoming a movie star can enjoy community theater work. Vernon, who wanted to be an auto racer and still harbors a secret desire to race cars, now gets pleasure out of his model raceway. "I have a lot of fun with it," Vernon said, "and it is very relaxing. I have built a tabletop platform and made some of my own accessories. You know, model-racing requires skill, so I belong to a club now, and we have regular races." There are many ways we can work out these unfulfilled childhood fantasies that will make our adult lives happier.

SEXUALITY AND LEISURE

Few people are willing to admit that pornography is their hobby, and yet it does remain a full-time leisure activity for many persons, just as the active pursuit of women for sexual purposes is the hobby of some men who use all their spare time to meet women, court them, and if possible, make love to them. Of course, not all men who are interested in women as a hobby have this in mind as the sole purpose of their interest. Girl-watching is an old and enjoyable pastime, and in some locales and cultures it is indulged in as a part of the social ritual. In Mexico, for example, it is customary to have a parade of young people in the town plazas. The boys go in one direction, the girls in the opposite, around and around the plaza with much laughter and looking. In almost any country girl-watching could be characterized as a cultural sport, and although it certainly has elements of sexuality, its main purpose is the simple, unadulterated enjoyment of seeing pretty girls.

In another area the common practice of players in many sports—patting each other on the buttocks—makes some of the players and the spectators feel sexually stimulated. Also, one man admitted to me, "I like to play football because quite frankly I get a sexual thrill out of the sport, the contact I have with other men." This man was not an open homosexual but did have difficulty in having sexual relations with his wife. He reported that after playing or watching football he was able to have satisfactory sexual intercourse with her. This sexual stimulation may extend to the locker-room camaraderie where there is continued possibility for the satisfaction of latent homosexual tendencies.

The popularity of health spas and health gymnasiums is due at least partly to this same repressed desire to be in an intimate situation with members of the same sex. The nudity or near-nudity, which is often more sexually exciting, that is possible in the steam rooms, swimming pools, and other parts of the health clubs makes it possible for Mr. and Mrs. Average Citizen to satisfy that part of them that is titillated by and interested in homosexuality. For the active homosexual it is a way of also satisfying certain impulses and in some cases of making contacts with others who might be interested in forming a sexual relationship.

In leisure, as in any other part of life, sex has its place and its purpose, but an overemphasis on sexual matters during leisure is a sign of personality deficiency.

WHEN TELEVISION TAKES OVER

No other medium has called forth such a mixture of praise and blame as has television. In an interview in 1969 Nicholas Johnson, a Federal Communications Commissioner, stated that in his opinion television was causing increased mental illness, alcoholism, drug addiction, violence, and unhappy family relationships. Dr. S. I. Hayakawa, president of San Francisco State College, blamed television for the increase in violence among young people whom he referred to as the "television generation." And other experts claim that today's people are becoming overweight and lazy because they spend so much time watching television. It has become the "in" thing to refer to the television set as the "boob tube," and yet some people claim that television has brought not only entertainment but education into the homes of millions. Buckminster Fuller says that the rise in world literacy is due to first the radio and now television. Who is right? Is television the great panacea, or is it a plague? As a psychiatrist I would say that it is a rather complicated mixture of both and that the trouble lies not so much with the set as with the viewer. When television takes over, as it has been allowed to do in the majority of homes, the human personality and intellect can become stunted. The fact that is often ignored is that no one has to watch television. There is no coercion to turn on the family set and leave it on from early morning until the late-night show, yet there certainly seems to be some compulsion to do so. In many homes the television set is the other member of the family, and sometimes it gets closer attention than any person in the house.

Television-viewing offers some interesting revelations about personality characteristics. You choose what you view because that program satisfies some need. The soap operas form the major interest of a large number of viewers who would not think of missing any of them. I have heard the fictional characters portrayed on these shows discussed with a seriousness and concern that far outweighed any interest the viewer had shown in the actual people around him. Often those who are most devoted to the soap opera are people with problems in their own lives but who are unwilling to face those problems. Those who are accident-prone and crisis-oriented enjoy these shows because they bear out their contention that accidents and misfortunes can happen to anyone. "Why blame me for the things that happen to me?" is what they are saying; "Just look at what happens to those people!" In some instances the soap opera serves as a substitute for life for viewers who cannot face either the dullness of their own existence or their unresolved emotional problems. It acts as a catharsis when they watch the story of someone in trouble who either solves the problem or has it replaced by a new situation. Lonely people like the soap opera because it gives them a ready-made group of people in whom they can be interested and about whom they know everything. This is the same reason these programs appeal to the gossip: It is an acceptable form of voyeurism, and the viewer can discuss without censure the lives and peccadilloes of the characters. Incidentally, watching these programs is not confined solely to women; men who have the time and the same emotional outlook become as engrossed in the programs as women do. I know of several cases where the husband comes home for lunch so that he and his wife can watch the programs together.

Highly aggressive and competitive people like to watch programs in which there is a high incidence of violence: mystery shows, police-crime shows, horror movies, and westerns in which there is a maximum amount of shooting. Older people

and people who are uninformed about and little
interested in the state of the world prefer to
watch variety shows and family-situation com-
edies which are asexual in nature and in which
everything always turns out all right. That is, the
problem, which was minor to begin with, is always
solved by the end of thirty or sixty minutes. All
the families portrayed are loving and kind. There
are no lasting problems related to poverty, disease,
or violence. Even with color sets the world is art-
fully reduced to a simple black-and-white value
system in which the good is easily distinguished
from the bad, and the good always emerges vic-
torious.

If you are a hypochondriac and worry about
your health, the shows you will most enjoy watching are the many programs that deal with medical
problems. You may even give your family phy-
sician a rest while you become engrossed in the
medical world as portrayed by Marcus Welby and
other television "doctors." Edna formerly spent
much of her time and a great deal of her husband's money on unnecessary visits to doctors
and hospitals. Although she had been told she
had no real health problem, Edna continued to
have a constantly changing variety of symptoms.
She still has her symptoms, but now she gets
relief by watching the medical programs on television. "Television doctors," she explains, "tell me
more about medicine and disease than my own
doctors ever did! I just wish that I could find a
nice friendly doctor that is as good as some of the
ones on TV!" In the meantime Edna is able to go
on a medical binge each week and have a new and
(to her) delightful disease.

Television could be a help in improving the

quality of our lives, but it has instead brought out personality traits of apathy, lack of realistic orientation to life situations, a preference for doing nothing, and a steadily growing introversion. A science-fiction writer once described a world of the future in which each person lived in isolation, communicating only through television screens and seeing the world only through the screens. This was meant to occur far, far in the future, but there are already people who live that way. All they see and experience comes to them from a small and powerful box. They have lost their desire and their capacity to observe life firsthand. Their personalities have been shaped and drained of significance by a mechanical device.

ART, MUSIC, AND PERSONALITY

The twin cultural interests of art and music account for the leisure hours of many in the form of actual participation or in the more passive role of viewer or listener. Your preferences in these areas, too, offer clues about your personality. If you prefer art that lacks recognizable form and is fragmented, you are saying that your life is similarly without purpose and plan. You are giving clues to your hidden anxieties and tensions. If you choose pictures that are very formal, you are probably a person who puts an emphasis on rules and strict standards of behavior. You do not approve of what you call flights of fancy, and you would like to see everything kept within bounds. A preference for the art of the past shows a disenchantment with the modern world and the technology it represents. On the other hand if you fill your home with pop art, you are saying to other people, "Look, I am a person of today, and I like the modern world, including its materialism and commercialism." If you hang primitives on your wall, you are showing that you do not think that training and study are important. You still believe in the philosophy of the self-made man and think the act of accomplishment greater than skill.

Mr. and Mrs. Jones have their walls hung with reproductions of the lush paintings of Renoir, Gauguin, and similar artists. These paintings gratify the orally centered Joneses, who also like to live in warm, comfortable surroundings crowded with over-stuffed furniture. By way of contrast their neighbors, the Andersons, have hung reproductions of stark paintings such as those by Mondrian. The Andersons like straight lines and simple designs with clean-cut edges. They are not interested in creature comforts, and their house is meticulously kept and sparsely furnished. Their approach to life is intellectual rather than sensual.

Your musical preferences can indicate whether your personality is an oral one, a depressive or aggressive one, a well-adjusted one, or one that consists of a combination of personality traits. The romantic who thinks of love as "making the world go round" will like to listen to songs that celebrate love. Many songs popular with young people are concerned with love themes, since love is an almost constant preoccupation with the adolescent. Music is a part of the courtship ritual, and most couples have a favorite love song which they refer to as "our song." If you like songs that are sentimental and wish-fulling, you are not particularly realistic about yourself or your life. You still believe in magic and happy endings without any effort on your part to make your dreams come true.

Persons who have been reared in strict homes and who are unable to take a relaxed attitude toward sexual matters will often get a form of release through listening to songs that have sexual implications. These songs, which they characterize as "naughty," are to them like writing dirty words on walls; they would consider the latter juvenile behavior, whereas they accept the songs as being a form of adult entertainment.

Aggressive individuals enjoy band music, very intellectual people prefer string quartets, persons with strong ego desires like concertos in which the individual artist is featured, and oral personalities prefer the full orchestrations of the symphony. To people who feel alienated from society and themselves, electronic music expresses their own lack of human contacts and life rhythm. The "no harmony, no melody" school of such composers as John Cage symbolizes the breakdown in modern human communications and relationships.

Music more than any other art is a kind of emotional shorthand which can be used to evoke as well as express a mood. Music helps some people find relief from tension and stress; it allows the inhibited to express feelings and emotions satisfactorily. How you use music is also highly significant in terms of your personality and its development. If you need music to help you get through the day, there is something wrong with your life. Using music as a constant buffer between you and the world indicates a lack of personal adjustment.

Getting a vicarious sexual experience by listening to sensual music and suggestive lyrics also indicates a lack of adjustment. If you use music to get emotional relief from tension, it may be serving a useful purpose provided that you do not lean too heavily on it. If you do, you should try to discover the cause of your emotional tension and cope with the problem directly. Music like any form of the arts can reflect life but should not become a substitute for it.

BOOKS AND PERSONALITY

Aldous Huxley said, "The proper study of mankind is books." A psychologist would say that the study of an individual can begin with the books he reads. Books are an extension of the personality and a reflection of the thoughts and emotions within that personality. Books are very close to the person who is reading them. They may be read for entertainment, education, or emotional satisfaction. They may be used to close out an unfriendly world or open windows into a wider one. What you choose to read, why you read, and what you get from books all reveal things about your personality.

Reading is a solitary act, and for that reason it often becomes the main leisure-time activity for individuals who are timid and lack a sense of social adjustment. They may be actually afraid of real people and human contacts and prefer to make friends with fictional characters, to live vicariously through the exploits of either imaginary people or real people from history with whom they cannot be personally acquainted. If you have more friends in books than you have in real life, you are afraid to risk your emotions in a relationship with another person. This may be because you have suffered some earlier disappointment or traumatic experience in your dealings with others; or you may distrust other people and know that at least the people you read about won't let you down. You have a poor self-image and feel inadequate, so you borrow from literature the personality characteristics that you feel you lack. But no amount of reading is going to supply the personality traits you lack, nor will you learn basic patterns of adjustment. You may be very well read but have difficulty in coping with interpersonal relations.

The individual who reads little or who reads comic books is intellectually and emotionally impoverished. His world is a simple two-dimensional one with no room for philosophy or theory. More advanced than this, though not much, are people who read light stories of the "fairy tale" type. Many of these readers are frustrated in their lives, and they look to stories for happy endings. Mrs. C. had a domestic problem and was on the verge of losing her husband. Instead of trying to solve her own problem, she spent her time reading confession magazines in which stories of domestic trouble always had a satisfactory ending. Incidentally, one of the causes of Mrs. C.'s marriage problems was her inability to be realistic about life. She lived in a world that only existed between the pages of her favorite magazines, and her husband could no longer tolerate this behavior. In his words, "I want a wife who is a woman, not a kid mooning over some love story!"

It is characteristic of children and adolescents to try to satisfy their curiosity about life through reading. They are trying to get some experience of various life situations. This is normal and useful in their progression toward adulthood, but there must come a time when they have an urge to experience these things for themselves. Many circumstances must be experienced firsthand if full adult maturation is to be reached. Books serve as guides for young people and should be a part of their leisure-time activities; as such, books form a part of what we might call modern puberty rites.

Adventure stories are popular with the timid, for in them they can pretend that they are doing things that in real life they would never have the courage to do. People may also like science fiction for the adventure element, although it may also appeal to those with a hidden fear of the future. Modern life and the coming future frighten them, and yet they have a compulsion to read about them. They especially enjoy stories in which men are able to defeat machines. Westerns have a special appeal for the city man who has never been to the open spaces. These stories satisfy his needs for a primitive way of life. He can be virile and authoritarian in his mind, even though in real life he may be meek and henpecked. While he is reading, he can forget the crowded, noisy city life, his boss, his whining children, and his complaining wife as in his mind he rides off into the sunset, heart and soul with the heroic cowboy or outlaw gunslinger.

Violence in books has a special appeal for the person who has a high level of aggression. It is a safe and approved way of working out aggressive feelings. The man who would secretly like to murder his boss or his wife can get some satisfaction from reading a sadistic murder story. In fact, murder and crime stories help to let people drain off their antisocial impulses. For this very reason, incidentally, Bertrand Russell in his later years read about one detective novel a day. For people who are law-abiding but who think they might enjoy being crooks if they had the nerve, books such as *The Godfather* offer vicarious satisfaction.

It is mistakenly thought that people are led to commit acts of violence and sexual aggression because of the books they have read. The truth is that people already have these impulses of aggression, and they look for books that will cater to those drives. They seek out reading material that will allow them to reenact their fantasies in their minds. A girl is not led to promiscuous behavior because she reads stories with a sexual content; she has read the stories because she has such strong sexual desires. If no opportunity for actual realization of these desires presents itself or if she is too timid to carry out her desires, her sexual fantasies will continue to be satisfied by reading. But if she has a strong enough drive and a good opportunity to engage in sexual activities, she will do so. Moralists will blame the books found in her possession, but like the books read by criminals, they are not the cause of her misbehavior or antisocial acts but another facet of her personality-adjustment problem. One of the reasons for the popularity of *Portnoy's Complaint* was that it gave readers an opportunity to enjoy reading about another person's masturbation acts after having had to repress their own feelings about masturbation. It is not unusual for adolescents to masturbate while looking at books that contain sexual material. This is not abnormal; they are only trying to satisfy their natural sexual curiosity and drive. In a society that is, despite much permissiveness, still largely puritan in concept books often have to take the place of actual sexual experiences. Pornography in this respect is not leading people to sex and sexual acts; it is taking the place of sex and leading people away from actual sexual experiences. Pornography is a substitute act and an unsatisfactory one in terms of emotional development. The whole question of evil and sinfulness in books comes back to the basic fact that it is not the books that are to be blamed. Any wrongdoing or thoughts of wrongdoing are inherent in the reader's mind, and he uses books only to keep alive his already conceived fantasies. When thinking of books as "evil" influences, it is well to remember these words from Voltaire: "I know many books which have bored their readers, but I know of none which has done real evil."

Books are also used as a way of acting out positive fantasies. Thus, if you want to be successful and rich, you will read self-help and guidance books in your leisure time. You will use your leisure as a way in which to improve your circumstances. If you read biographies of famous people, you are showing a desire to model your own personality on the lives of those who have succeeded. If, however, you read the lives of the great only because you enjoy the scandal that may be connected with some episodes in their lives, you are showing peeping-tom characteristics. This very common attitude accounts for the great popularity and proliferation of magazines that publish so-called true stories about people in public life, especially movie and television stars. I once treated a woman whose personal life was unsatisfactory because her habit of gossiping had caused her to lose her husband and most of her friends. She read nothing but magazines and papers that contained gossip-type articles. When she did read a book, it had to be in the nature of an exposé of some important person. Another person I know had an insatiable curiosity about other people's private lives, and his favorite reading matter was collections of letters that famous people had written.

Books can give you motivation and move you and your plans forward, or they can allow you to live in fantasy without ever trying to carry out your plans. But books do not make you do anything; books are not your controllers. You use books in the same way you use any tool in directing the way in which your life should flow. Your choice of books to read, your personal library, tell what your hidden thoughts are and what your level of accomplishment is going to be.

Because leisure is such a large part of your time and since there is going to be an increasing amount available, the way in which you spend it is going to be more and more important to you. If you are going to be able to express yourself fully, you will want to understand what your leisure-time activities mean in terms of your total personality. Leisure should be flexible and should be a time not only of fun and enjoyment but also of growing.

The habits that you develop during your leisure time are habits that reveal your supposedly hidden personality, and that personality is revealed not only by what you do for fun but by what you don't do and how you feel about leisure in general. Looking at your leisure is a way to see what you are trying to do with your life. You may be using hobbies and forms of recreation to avoid the meaningful confrontations of life. You may be using your leisure as a time of creative expression. The way to decide whether or not your leisure time is being invested in the best way is to add up what dividends you are receiving. If you are getting back happiness, emotional satisfaction, increased self-esteem, and good interpersonal relationships, then you have a positive leisure-time program. It is just as important to you as a person to be successful in your leisure as you are in your work, and often the two go together.

Leisure habits as well as the other habits and attitudes that you have are inseparable from you. They are part of your life-long voyage of self-discovery, a voyage that you yourself chart for navigation. Your habits are as distinctive as your fingerprints, and they tell the world what kind of a person you are. If your habits are a kind of mirror that reflects your personality, it is a mirror that has an advantage that no other mirror has: The image can be changed! This is an emotional and psychological advantage because you know that your personailty can be altered, and to do this you have only to change your habits and attitudes. This knowledge gives you a freedom that other creatures can never possess. You are a multiple and clever organism which can change and alter both yourself and your surroundings. That is, you have this vital capacity, but you still have to decide to use it. As H. G.

Wells said: "Man is today a challenged animal. He has to respond, he has to respond successfully to the challenge, or he will be overwhelmed—like any other insufficiently adaptable animal."

Index

195

ABOUT THE AUTHOR

As resident psychiatrist at the Detroit Receiving Hospital, DR. JEAN ROSENBAUM became expert at making quick emergency diagnoses of personalities on the bases of habits, gestures, choices, opinions, and so forth. The insights he gained there, and in seventeen years as a practicing psychiatrist, enabled him to write this book. Dr. Rosenbaum has had an illustrious and varied career in medicine, in psychiatry, and as a technical consultant (for TIME magazine, among other publications); he has also published several volumes of poetry (he received the Hart Crane Poetry Award in 1965). He has published hundreds of articles on psychiatry for the general audience.

Bantam
On Psychology

IN AND OUT THE GARBAGE PAIL by Frederick S. Perls, M.D., Ph.D. (DM7299—$1.65)

GESTALT THERAPY VERBATIM by Frederick S. Perls, M.D., Ph.D. (DM7292—$1.65)

BLACK RAGE by William Grier & Price Cobbs. Two Negro Psychiatrists examine the Negro mentality in this brilliant best seller. (N3931—95¢)

BEYOND THE PLEASURE PRINCIPLE by Sigmund Freud. (NM5381—95¢)

THE REVOLUTION OF HOPE by Erich Fromm analyzes the problems and hopes of mankind in a mechanized society. (N4187—95¢)

PSYCHOANALYSIS AND RELIGION by Erich Fromm. (NM5558—95¢)

THE FIFTY-MINUTE HOUR by Robert Lindner. The brilliant study of psychosis and violence. (QM7208—$1.25)

We Deliver!
And So Do These Bestsellers.

LISTEN!

We represent world-famous authors (many published by Bantam), newsmakers, personalities and entertainers who know how to grab and hold an audience's attention and at the same time, make them enjoy listening. And their fees fit many budgets.

So if you, or someone you know, sets up discussions, debates, forums, symposiums or lectures you should get in touch with us.

We're the BANTAM LECTURE BUREAU and we'll send you a free copy of our catalog which will tell you exactly who we represent and what they talk about.

To get your copy simply fill out the coupon below and mail it to:

BANTAM LECTURE BUREAU
Dept. BLB-1
666 Fifth Avenue
New York, N.Y. 10019

My organization plans_____programs each year.

NAME_____

COLLEGE/ASSOCIATION_____

ADDRESS_____

CITY_____STATE/ZIP_____

BLB1—7/73

If you need information in a big hurry, just call us 212-245-8172

Your World, The REAL Way!

Six helpful, to-the-point guides that give you everything you need to know **before** you go and while you're there. No matter how many times you've been there these guides compiled by local experts, are invaluable.

FREE!
Bantam Book Catalog

It lists over a thousand money-saving best-sellers originally priced from $3.75 to $15.00 —bestsellers that are yours now for as little as 50¢ to $2.25!

The catalog gives you a great opportunity to build your own private library at huge savings!

So don't delay any longer—send for your catalog TODAY! It's absolutely FREE!
